I0505111

The M.S. Dhoni Way

Leadership Master Class from the

Master of the Craft…

@9000RPM Publishing Works

RAJAT NARANG

BHUMIKA CHANDRA

Also by the Authors:

Airbus vs. Boeing: Strategy Wars, Tactical Dogfights, High-G
Maneuvers and the Photo Finishes – 1970s to 2020 – Rajat Narang

Birds of Fray – World's Top 4.5 & 5th Gen Fighter Jet Aircraft Programs

Birds of Fray – Top Gun Maverick: Special dition

Phoenix Junction: The Cauldron of Inner Alchemy – By Bhumika
Chandra

Copyright © 2023 Rajat Narang & Bhumika Chandra

All rights reserved.

The right of Rajat Narang & Bhumika Chandra to be identified as the Co-Authors of this work has been asserted in accordance with the Copyright Act, 1957. This work is further protected under Berne Convention for Protection of Literary and Artistic Works, 1886 and the Universal Copyrights Convention.

All rights reserved. No part of this publication may be reproduced in any form or by any electronic or mechanical means including information storage and retrieval systems without obtaining prior written permission. The content is being provided for personal utilization only and redistribution or further circulation in any form or by any means, including, storage on internet on publicly accessible web pages is strictly prohibited.

Published by: @9000RPM Publishing Works

Cover Page Design: Canva.com

Cover Image Credits: BCCI under Editorial Usage

DEDICATED TO

MSD Himself for being a Lighthouse of Humility, Virtues & True Leadership having lived them for almost 2 decades now...

Image Credits: © S. Lakshmanan aka Latchu
https://latchuart.wordpress.com/

Disclaimer

The Authors do not have any kind of financial investments, direct or indirect business associations or financial stakes of any sort in MSD or any of the companies or businesses owned, run or promoted by him. This work does not promote or endorse any particular individual, company or industry OEM & its products over others in any manner whatsoever.

The opinions expressed throughout are purely authors' personal and the views & judgments presented are neither directed or targeted at anyone nor meant as pontification of any sort and are solely based on objective assessment of the subject matter. The names of products, systems and/or brand names mentioned wherever through the work are intellectual property of their respective owners and their mention has been done only & purely for information & creative purposes and it does not indicate or reflect and should not be construed as any kind of endorsement or promotion of any kind. The authors do not have any direct business association with any of the mentioned leadership theorists, authors & other domain specialists of past or present and do not have any commercial stakes involved in any of their works or publications.

The work intends to provide a structural analysis of the leadership strategies, practices developed, cultivated & pursued by MSD on the field. The contents are not intended at chronicling his life, career events or glorification of achievements etc. in any broad or specific ways from a fan-boy's perspective. The intent has been to provide objective analysis based on facts from the perspective of leadership against the light of some of the existing, most prominent leadership theories by some of the pre-eminent domain scholars while firmly toeing the thin line of objectivity right in the middle without getting awed by the fanfare or swayed by the criticism. The leadership context presented here has tactical leadership as the core pivot with focus on small, specialized & high performance teams.

All the information, data & facts presented herein have been derived from reliable secondary sources, reasonably verified & have been presented for informational purposes only All effort & due diligence has been done to ensure the accuracy of the same, however, the same can't be guaranteed. The views & opinions expressed throughout have been presented in light of the supporting facts & evidences by duly citing the sources alongside. Feel free to write in case of any concerns. The relevant jurisdiction in case of any judicial intervention would solely be New Delhi.

The presented content contains generic information only and is not suitable for addressing specific or particular circumstances of any specific case or scenario. The content, thus, is not intended to be used as a basis for taking decisions of commercial or any other nature. The authors and the publisher disclaim all liabilities originating from the outcomes of the application of the contents in real-life scenarios without duly conducting thorough due diligence and without seeking professional advice & opinion from relevant subject matter experts.

CONTENTS

Dedicated to

Preface

Introduction

Preface

It was August 15, 2020 with the first ever lockdown in the 21st century (owing to pandemic) having already forced everyone to be truly home bound and jaded. A message appeared on the Instagram and the news it contained suddenly spread like wildfire on the social media which was abuzz with activity as well as news channels across the length & breadth of the country. It was from the nation's heartthrob MS Dhoni who had announced his retirement from international cricket with a cryptic message, "From this day on consider me retired", leaving millions of his fans across the globe incapacitated, in disarray and almost petrified with shock. The message instantly dashed the hopes of millions to see their hero back donning the Team India's blue jersey after almost a year of him having not played international cricket, since the semi-final of the ODI World Cup of 2019 held in England, wherein, his unfortunate run out against New Zealand had actually led to India's exit from the tournament while also heralding the beginning of the end of a long & illustrated career of a highly decorated legend of Indian cricket.

Everyone wanted a great farewell for their beloved MSD from international cricket; everyone wanted him to leave at a good note after the heartbreak of WC 2019 which had still been paining a year later. We all wanted to do something for him but alas we were helpless and could do nothing. The writing was there on the wall that it was time for him to finally hang his boots & the gloves. Amid those turbulent & tumultuous moments marked by an unstoppable emotional roller coaster of sorts, a duo of his ardent fans decided to write a book on MSD and about the most impactful aspect of his on-field presence, which could also easily be termed as his ultimate legacy, and that's his leadership. The endeavor was intended as a fitting tribute to the man who came, homed-in and conquered everyone's heart & every conceivable trophy & award in the cricketing world becoming the only soul on the planet to have won the triple crown of cricket, namely, the ICC's 2007 T20 WC, the 2011's ODI WC and the 2013's Champions Trophy.

He also developed a comprehensive system & process geared towards winning, pivoted around complete situational awareness & contextual ownership, transformational leadership of the team with his unique leadership style (with camaraderie & patented coolness on & off the field as hallmarks), transparency, inclusivity & engagement apart from a hawkish game control on the field marked by decisive as well as precise, critical calls. All of these collectively have duly earned him the sobriquet of 'Captain Cool' and the well deserved respect of his teammates, praise of authorities & media, envy of his competitors and deification with an almost god-like fan-following which has stayed intact even after his formal retirement from international cricket. This is besides a collection of hard to beat statistics & records for the record book as captain & with the bat which are likely to stay in the annals of Indian cricket for a very long time to come.

Our intent here has been not to write a eulogy of any kind for glorification or appeasement from a typical fan's perspective or for a 'fan boy' or 'fan girl' moment but rather to actually study & decrypt his leadership process & the method to the mega successful madness of the cricketing genius which has had a tremendous impact & influence on the way the sport is played in our country.

Being from the Learning & Development (L&D) and Research domains respectively apart from being hardcore cricket & MSD fans for decades, we were uniquely qualified and in a perfect position to approach the subject from a distinctive professional as well as personal perspective. The approach undertaken was to decrypt MSD's on-field approaches, methodologies and operating concepts, as exhibited on-field since taking over the reins of the Indian Cricket team in September 2007, in the light of existing domain literature and leadership theories as the guiding beacon to derive insights and actual, actionable learning principles which could be applied directly by existing as well as budding leaders and anyone to inspire and drive their teams to peak performance while realizing their true potential.

The approach undertaken has been to structure each chapter around the following 5 pillars:-

1. A unique, core underlying leadership concept as well as its theoretical underpinnings

2. The working or functional methodology of the concept answering 'Why & how it works'

3. Application of the same by MSD & others on the cricket field with actual quoted examples

4. Concept's application in other sports apart from business world & military leadership as caselets

5. Deriving the ultimate learning principle as a distilled outcome of the entire iterative learning process

Here is that work in its final, ultimate form having undergone a series of mutations, ageing and maturation over the years coming as a gift from two ardent MSD fans to MSD himself and to his millions of true fans across the globe as his true & lasting legacy…

Hope it proves to be useful and achieves its intended objectives…

Introduction

It was a pleasant spring day on April 05, 2005 in Visakhapatnam with the venue being the Dr. Y.S. Rajasekhara Reddy ACA-VDCA Cricket Stadium where a cricket match was being played between the traditional arch-rivals, India and Pakistan. The ODI was the second match of the six match ODI series with Pakistan touring India. The Indian skipper, Sourav Ganguly, won the toss and elected to bat first with India's opening pair of Sachin Tendulkar and Virender Sehwag taking on the Pakistan fast bowlers. The fourth over of India's innings turned out to be eventful for Pakistan with Sachin Tendulkar getting run out on a throw from Yousuf Youhana at a personal score of just 2 runs off the 8 balls he played.

It was a big blow for India with Sachin having been dismissed cheaply. However, everyone was surprised to see the player who walked out of the dressing room to play at number 3. He was a wearing the number 7 jersey with long, flowing hair and an unmistakable, flamboyant appearance. The jersey read the name as M.S. Dhoni, which many had not come to recognize by then. However, their lack of recognition was going to be ephemeral with the same going to last just a single day as a new star was going to be born in Visakhapatnam that day.

Dada's (Sourav Ganguly) decision to send a rookie Dhoni at number 3 was highly unusual given the star studded nature of the Indian batting line-up. However, the radical call was borne more out of Dada's calculative mind with him wanting India to take-off right at the outset of the innings to be able to make the most of the pitch conditions. Further, he wanted

Dhoni to have more time to play out there in the field as he had batted lower down the batting order in his four previous innings in international cricket without any real impact, especially, in India's tour of Bangladesh of 2004. For Dhoni, coming out first down was his preferred batting position given that he had been batting at number 3 only in first class cricket. Dhoni took the guard and got off the mark with a boundary coming of an elegant off-drive.

In a subsequent double whammy for Pakistan bowlers, the power hitting duo of Virender Sehwag & MS Dhoni smacked them real hard to all corners of the ground with a partnership of 96-run forming between them in just over 10 overs. Sehwag, however, unfortunately lost out on his century by getting out at the score of 74.

His dismissal brought Dravid on to the field and 'The Wall' provided Dhoni, the man on a demolition mission, enough stability at the other end to continue his decimation of a beleaguered bowling attack muscling fours and sixes in quick succession. In an impressive & outstanding display of belligerence, skilled stroke-play and firepower; Dhoni made his maiden century and finished his innings with a big hundred, making 148 runs, which came off just 123 balls. This included 15 fours & 4 huge sixes, of which, two of them were clobbered savagely over long-off.

India ultimately made 356 runs in their assigned 50 overs that day, thereby, setting a daunting target for the visitors to chase & win which they just couldn't manage to do. India won the match by 58 runs with Dhoni named as the player of the match.

Dhoni, thus, had arrived and announced his arrival in style with an awesome display of fireworks in a traditional, high-stakes arch-rivalry in front of a cheering home crowd. In the post-match presentation, Dada said,

"When I looked at the wicket in the morning it looked like it would crumble quite quickly, and might not even be good for batting for the first 50 overs. So the toss was absolutely crucial, and once we won it, it was important that we made as many runs as possible in the first 15 overs. That's why we made the decision to send Dhoni in and he played fantastically well."[1]

Dhoni provided a quick glimpse of his precocious talent and the shape of things to come in his statement made in the post match presentation. He said, "After I got to a hundred I felt it was important to push the scoring as much as possible so that we could make about 350. The ball was not doing anything off the pitch and I knew that even a score of 350 might not be enough."[1]

An article appearing in media the same day was headlined "A man possessed" [2] with the first paragraph of the article reading out as, "When Mahendra Singh Dhoni left the field today after having lashed 148 in only his fifth innings in international cricket, he had imprinted such an array of astounding strokes on the memory of those watching that a dozen knowledgeable observers could have each picked a personal favourite and no two choices need have been the same"[2]. It further had a piece of advice meant for the selectors in a caption, which read, "Mahendra Singh Dhoni's stunning 148 should finally settle the debate over India's wicketkeeper-batsman in ODIs" [2]. And yes, the debate & the quest both were settled & the position was sealed with a crackerjack of a performance.

Marking one's arrival with a debut or a rocking performance against Pakistan surely has been a dream come true for some other cricketers as well prior to Dhoni with the pack led by none other than the master blaster, Sachin Tendulkar, himself. Sachin made his test debut against Pakistan in

November 1989 at the tender age of 16 while facing the pace battery of Imran Khan and Wasim Akram with the match played at Karachi. His ODI debut also was against Pakistan, a month later in December 1989, with the venue being Sharjah for the shorter format of the game. The key difference, however, was that Sachin got to his maiden century in his 79th game and after a span of almost of 5 years in 1994 against Australia in Colombo. However, it took him only 8 test matches to get to his first test century coming against England in 1990 at the age of 17 while batting in tricky English conditions.

Indian opener Navjot Singh Sidhu also made his maiden ODI century against Pakistan at the Champions Trophy played at Sharjah in October 1989. Sidhu made 108 of 121 balls, however, India ended up being on the losing side despite having put a score of 273 on the board while batting first. Sidhu's maiden century came after 2 years of having made his ODI debut against Australia in October 1987.

Virender Sehwag, another explosive Indian batsman, too, made his ODI debut vs. Pakistan in April 1999. However, he also took a span of over 2 years to reach his maiden ODI century made against New Zealand of just 69 balls in August 2001.

However, against this backdrop, Dhoni's maiden century coming in just his fifth ODI inning spoke volumes about and almost proved to be a harbinger of what destiny had in store for him and what he had in store for India and the nation's beloved game…

Fast forward to now in IPL 2023, exactly 19 years later with MSD being a living legend of the game, nothing much has changed except the fact that every stadium across the country has become MSD' home ground with chants of 'Dhoni', 'Dhoni' and the crescendo of spectators' cheering when he comes out for the toss or to bat having become many times louder.

The Star Sports commentator Danny Morrison asked a much older version of M.S. Dhoni at the outset of an IPL fixture about his retirement saying that he believed it was his last IPL tournament to which a cheeky & evasive MSD replied that it's his (Danny) decision & judgment on his IPL career rather than being his own to which Danny announced much to the delight of the crowd that MSD will be playing next year's IPL as well to which the ecstatic crowd erupted in a loud roar of rapture. Such scenes have been very common in the IPL 2023 with the crowds thronging stadiums across the nation for every CSK match donning yellow jerseys just to capture a mere glimpse of MSD and to cheer for every four & six hit by him. Further, CSK's game against KKR at the Eden Gardens virtually looked like it was taking place in CSK's home ground with the spectator stands looking like the yellow sea with almost everyone donning the yellow jersey and MSD quipping in the post match presentation, "They all have come in yellow to bid farewell to me as I am in the last phase of my career, however, long I may play." The feeling was felt once again following the lap of honour taken by Dhoni and the entire CSK team & support staff in Chennai following CSK's last home game for IPL 2023 at Chepauk was overwhelming & almost unforgettable with tennis balls and jerseys being distributed to fans by Dhoni with a heartfelt thanks and the legend of the game Mr. Sunil Gavaskar suddenly appearing in front of the camera covering MSD to take Dhoni's autograph on his shirt and then giving Dhoni a real warm hug. That's the magic of MSD which simply refuses to fade away…

The cricket commentator and former cricketer Mr. Aakash Chopra has rightly & aptly put it, "MSD is not just a player or name but rather an emotion and a sentiment" and it will always remain so…

CHAPTER – I

THE COMPLETE OWNERSHIP CULTURE – CREATING A CULTURE OF TAKING OWNERSHIP INSTEAD OF BLAME GAMES

It was a match between RCB and KKR in the IPL 2023 held at the M Chinnaswamy Stadium in Bangalore in April 2023. Virat Kohli, the stand-in skipper for the RCB won the toss and chose to field first looking to capitalize on Mohammed Siraj's ferocious pace to take quick wickets and restricting KKR to a reasonable total. However, KKR got to a flying start and managed to post a score of 200 on the board. While chasing, RCB managed to get to only 179/8 with some sloppy fielding, dropped chances and questionable shot selection by the batsmen. In the post match presentation, a visibly riled Virat Kohli had some tough words for his team. He said, "We handed them over the game. We deserved to lose because we were not professional enough on the field. The bowlers hit decent areas, but we didn't hold on to our chances. That's what you call a freebie in T20 cricket, and we literally handed them a victory there which is not ideal. We take pride in the way we play and tonight we were not up to standard and we're certainly not too shy to admit (it)".

That's a typical statement from a leader who believes in and practices complete ownership of himself and his team's performances on and off the field. And this is not the first time that we have seen him doing that. He has been doing it consistently and practiced even when he was the captain of the Indian cricket team from 2016 to late 2021. When a leader does this, he/she in-turn creates a culture of complete ownership, wherein, every player takes full responsibility for his performances and when that happens magic happens because the team culture becomes a complete ownership and learning culture.

Why Taking Ownership Works?

Two Ex-Navy SEAL officers of the U.S. Navy, named, Jocko Willink and Leif Babin have coined and defined the term called 'Extreme Ownership'[9] in their titular, bestselling leadership book as, "Taking complete ownership & full responsibility of the situation irrespective of the outcome"[9].

This principle of extreme ownership, outlined by Jocko and Leif, has been a distillation of their long & tough years of military service across Iraq's bloody battlefields, under the allied war on terror, which followed the tragic events of 9/11. However, its scope of application simply can't be restricted to the chaotic battlefields of military warfare with the same having equal relevance for the cricket field as well as business circles.

When a leader exercises complete & extreme ownership, irrespective of the fallout, it instills a sense of immense personal responsibility & accountability through the rank & file with everyone guided by that internal moral compass. When that happens, it creates a culture of constant improvement, high performance & betterment which accepts failures as an integral part of the process, instead of a culture of blame-game & finding scapegoats, which is simply disastrous, as it hinders the process of learning & improvement.

Further, as per the 6-steap change cycle or change acceptance cycle, which starts with shock/disbelief stage typically and subsequently goes through Denial, Fear, Grief/Sadness & Bargaining before finally reaching Acceptance. Acceptance, thus, is the last stage at which the change starts to take effect and the sooner that stage is reached by accepting failure the quicker it for anyone to change things effectively.

A Harvard Business Review Article, titled, Why You Should Take the Blame, says that, "Taking the blame serves as an example. When you take the blame, others get embarrassed about not taking the blame themselves. Being defensive makes you slippery. Taking responsibility makes you trustworthy. When they see you don't get shot, they feel emboldened to take the risk."[99] It further says, "It takes courage to own your blame, and that shows strength to accept failure. It immediately silences anyone who might try to blame you — what's the point if you've already taken the blame? The "blame you" conversation is over. Now you can focus on solving problems."[99]

The Blame Culture and Boeing's Self-Created 737MAX Crisis

The blame culture stands exactly 360 degrees opposite to the complete ownership culture, wherein, the leader instead of taking responsibility for the outcomes looks for scapegoats to put the blame on as a means to get away and it creates a culture of insecurity, mediocrity & stagnation, wherein, everyone just wants to play safe and save their jobs which effectively stifles new learning, initiatives or risk taking of any kind. The acquisition of McDonnell Douglas (MD) by Boeing in the late 1990s, with MD operating under a vastly different operating culture dominated by profits than Boeing, led to a major deterioration of Boeing's organizational culture with a subsequent shift towards profit orientation, after key MD executives took leadership positions within Boeing; in a key departure from Boeing's original engineering & quality focused culture earlier.

It led to a complete shift in Boeing's overarching focus towards prioritization of shareholder returns instead of investments towards the company's long term future leading to drastic cutbacks in Boeing's R&D expenditure towards development of new aircraft programs. For instance, the 737 program, which was designed in the mid-1960s and has been the bedrock of Boeing's single aisle market presence, has been in continuous service with periodic updates for almost over half a century now. Boeing's decision to further push the 737 platform beyond its limits with the decision to re-engine it once again in 2011 to compete with Airbus' A320neo program without getting the airplane re-certified by the FAA effectively precipitated the 737MAX disaster, marked by two subsequent air crashes which killed 346 people, put Boeing's credibility as a company on the line with numerous lawsuits & investigations that followed apart from creating a debt mountain for the company which went up from $20 billion prior to the crisis to $60 billion.

The entire blame for an inglorious and almost a catastrophic episode in Boeing's corporate history was squarely placed on the reigning CEO Dennis Muilenburg, the Chief Test Pilot and the head of Boeing's commercial airplanes division with the company still trudging & sleepwalking on a similar pathway while waiting for another disaster to wake up which might become too late. It is a perfect example of and almost a case study on how atrocious leadership, with utter lack of ownership &

responsibility can lead a ship, en route a path of mediocrity, eventually to a nearly fatal shipwreck.

MSD and the Culture of Complete Ownership

Interestingly, MSD, has been the paradoxical mix of the two above, being the ex-captain of the Indian cricket team as well as a military man having been in the trenches & holding the honorary rank of Lt. Col. in the Territorial Army unit of the Parachute Regiment of the Indian Army since 2011. Maybe that's why it comes naturally to him to take complete ownership of the team and its performances which has been easily evident and has been on display over the years with the skipper taking full responsibility of the team's downswings. On the contrary, upon winning trophies, it has invariably been the youngest players of the team holding them along with other members with Dhoni barely visible in the background.

The final of the 2011 ICC ODI World Cup was no exception to this and upon winning the cup, team India's celebrations seemed centered more on a celebration of Sachin Tendulkar's tremendous contribution to Indian cricket with the players hoisting him on their shoulders while taking the victory lap with MSD happily taking the backseat. Even English cricketer, Jos Buttler, expressed dismay at Dhoni's almost stoic & Spartan celebration act after winning the ODI World Cup of 2011 in a recent post on Cricbuzz.

He said, "I love the shot of him hitting that six to win the World Cup and then he twizzles his bat around. That was all he gave you. It is probably the biggest moment in Indian cricket history and he still just pulls it off with such composure. I love watching him play. I like that about him, made me intrigued about him. It is quite amazing trying to think what he is thinking about, why is he not riding the emotions of the game"[10].

The same has been true for the shortest format of the game in the league format, i.e. the IPLs, wherein as the captain of the Chennai Super Kings (CSK), MSD won the league title in 2010, 2011 and 2018. The 2020 season of the IPL, played in the UAE amid pandemic woes in India, however, was one of the worst seasons for CSK with the team clearly struggling throughout the tournament and finishing at the second last position on the points table for the first time ever losing 8 matches of the 14 total matches it played. MSD, however, in post match presentations, accepted complete ownership & responsibility for the team's dismal performances as the skipper following availability of limited practice opportunities prior to the tournament owing to COVID-19 related series of lockdowns & restrictions.

When CSK lost three matches in a row in the tournament, he said in the post match presentation, "Long time back since we lost three in a row. We need to get a lot of things right. It is the professionalism. We need to take our catches & not bowl no-balls. Those are the controllables and may-be we are getting too relaxed."[12]

Regarding his own performance with the bat, he was forthright in accepting, "I was not able to middle a lot of deliveries. Was trying to hit it too hard. When the wicket is slightly at the slower side, it is better to time it. Looking at outfield it was subconsciously coming to us to hit the ball hard,"[12]

This complete ownership of what had happened was accompanied by his alter-ego, the 'process', as well about which he was effusive in his repetitive rhetoric throughout the tournament. Some commentators & media even started writing his remaining cricketing career's unofficial obituary following that kind of performance from the CSK team, also labeled by some as the 'Dad's Army', given the high average age of players in the team. However, in the 2021 edition of the tournament; CSK staged a remarkable comeback, following a couple of changes in team composition & approach to the game; going to the second spot by the time the IPL 2021 was suspended indefinitely.

Another example of extreme ownership in action from MSD came in the just abandoned IPL 2021 held in India. When the players were to check out & depart from the team hotel following the suspension of the marquee event, MSD declared to the CSK team management, like the true captain of the ship in the popular tradition of the sea, that he would be the last one to leave the team hotel after CSK players get home safe. "Mahi bhai said that he will be the last person to leave the hotel. He wanted foreigners to leave first, then the Indian players. He will be taking the last flight tomorrow when everyone reaches their home safe and secure,"[11] as quoted by one of the CSK team members to the Indian Express.

Current Indian skipper, Virat Kohli, had the following to say about MSD. He said, while speaking to media prior to 2019's ODI World Cup, "There's one thing about MS that's far more important than anything else - and there's a lot to him - for him, the team is always above everything else. It's always about the team, no matter what."[86]

Gary Kirsten, who was the Indian team's coach during the 2011's World Cup win, had the following to say about Dhoni's ownership. He said, "I have read that great leaders in the world give credit to others when things are going well and take responsibility when things are going badly. MS Dhoni is that to the 'T'."[65]

Another popular quote from MSD, reminds one of his approach of practicing extreme ownership on the field. He said, "I need to blame myself. I am the leader of the side. I am the main culprit so of course I blame myself."[98]

Other Indian Skippers and Complete Ownership

It is not that MSD has been the only captain in the history of Indian cricket taking complete ownership of the team's vicissitudes, performances & outcomes. In fact, Ajinkya Rahane's captaincy of the Indian test team, during the 2020-2021's tour of Australia, as the stand-in skipper, would go down as one of the finest displays of leadership & captaincy; wherein, playing with inexperienced players amid injury woes to senior players, in front of hostile crowds hurling racist abuses under difficult & challenging playing conditions; he spearheaded India to a memorable victory in the test series against arch-rival, Australia after a crushing defeat in the opening test of the series.

Dada's complete & unflinching backing of India's spin ace, Anil Kumble; when the selectors wanted to drop him on India's tour of Australia in 2003 while mooting for a left-arm spinner; stands out as another example of taking complete & extreme ownership, as recounted by Dada in a webinar organized by UnAcademy in June 2020. He said, "I knew he was playing for his place. The selectors were clear that they didn't want him in the side and I put my foot down and said: he has to go because I knew this could be his end. The meeting went for couple of hours. In the end, I succeeded in getting Kumble to the flight to Australia. Before we left the country, the selectors said that if Kumble doesn't do well and India doesn't win, we will drop him first, before we drop anybody else. Kumble played that series, had a fantastic year. He ended that year with 75 wickets

— the most he had in his career in one season."[91]

Dada further said while sharing his precious pearls of leadership wisdom, "As a leader there will be times, when you would take easier options. Because when you play for a long period of time, everybody's career will not be the same — there will be highs, there will be lows. But I have believed, class is permanent and form is temporary. I knew the great Kumble had a little blip in his career and if you did not stand by him, we would lose one of the greatest of all times. He came out and went on to become a champion and even captained India after that."[91]

Complete Ownership Culture in the Business World

Another legend who vouched for, pursued & implemented the extreme ownership philosophy & culture in action fanatically, not in sports, but instead in the U.S. Aerospace & Defense industry in the 20th century; was the iconic & legendary U.S. airplane designer & aerospace genius, Clarence L. "Kelly" Johnson, who created & headed Lockheed Corporation's advanced research unit, Skunk Works, from post World War II to 1975. He designed & developed a number of masterpieces, namely, the U2 spy plane in 1950s, the F-100 Century series supersonic fighter jet in the 1960s. However, his magnum opus, as well as the world's fastest flying machine, the SR-71 Black Bird in the 1960s, which retains its speed records even to this day.

Kelly was the absolute authority on Skunk Works' operations throughout and always maintained that there should be a single head of operations of the specialized unit with complete authority. He also maintained that there must not be any bureaucratic interference into the Skunk's operations as it was established to work on high priority, confidential projects entailing complex & almost insurmountable engineering challenges while working along tight work schedules under numerous, high pressure deadlines for months altogether.

Rule 1of the 14 ground rules & practices formulated by Kelly for Skunk Works' operations, stated, that "The Skunk Works program manager must be delegated practically complete control of his program in all aspects. He should have the authority to make quick decisions regarding technical, financial or operational matters."[13] With his clearly laid out work rules, treated & followed with almost gospel like fervor, he always delivered on time with mind-boggling & top notch output always.

Interestingly, Kelly's ground rules & practices, developed first in the middle of the 20th century, are still at work and are still in use[22] at Skunk Works in 2021, almost 75+ years later by the small, highly empowered teams working at the Lockheed Martin's very same Skunk Works.

Ben Rich, Kelly's disciple & ultimate successor, who headed the Skunk Works from 1975 to 1991, has mentioned & summed up Kelly's approach to complete ownership in his personal memoir titled, Skunk Works, "Kelly ran Skunk Works as if it was his own, personal aerospace company"[13].

Learning Principle:

The leaders who work towards creating a culture of complete ownership effectively lay the foundation for the creation of a great team and organization which own up their mistakes as well as shortcomings, learns from them and works continuously striving towards improving and becoming an even better version of themselves every day. Contrastingly, teams and organizations which focus on blame shifting do not accept their limitations, shortcomings & weaknesses and thus do not change and improve over time, become stagnant and ultimately decay.

Chapter - II

TRANSFORMATIONAL LEADERSHIP – INSPIRING TO GO ABOVE & BEYOND THE CALL OF DUTY

The story & the journey of transformational leadership started with a single word, Charisma and its subsequent application in the leadership context. Charisma, etymologically, had its origin in the Greek root, Kharis, meaning favour, grace, charm. Thus, someone having the favour freely given or the gift of grace & charm was regarded as charismatic in the mid-17th century when the word came into the English language.

In the lexicon of leadership, Charismatic leadership's roots could be traced to the German sociologist, Max Weber's tripartite classification of authority which borrowed it from the theological context & generalized it. As per Weber, Charismatic Authority is a concept of leadership in which the authority is derived from the leader's charisma.

When someone talks about charismatic leaders, the first name that comes to mind from political leadership would be the 32nd American President, Franklin D. Roosevelt or the former British Prime Minister, Winston Churchill, both of whom leveraged their charisma, communication skills and connect with their people effectively to lead their respective countrymen through World War II which was one of the most difficult and almost existential crisis for the world. Churchill's 'Blood, Toil, Tears & Sweat' speech given to the House of Commons in May 1940 to set up realistic expectations in his inaugural speech as the wartime leader and the 'Victory at all costs' speech exhibited his character and characteristics to galvanize & mobilize a nation facing a brutal enemy. Contrastingly, the most prominent example from the business world would be Apple's founder & former CEO, Steve Jobs, with his charisma & influence.

Weber has defined charisma as, "a certain quality of an individual personality, by virtue of which he is set apart from ordinary men and treated as endowed with supernatural, superhuman, or at least specifically exceptional powers or qualities. These are such as are not accessible to the ordinary person, but are regarded as of divine origin or as exemplary, and on the basis of them the individual concerned is treated as a leader"[14].

As per Weber, this charisma, emanating from his aura of mysticism, creates a cult-like following for the leader in the followers and the phenomenon is highly sustainable with history showing that regimes based on charismatic leadership last the longest. A similar phenomenon has been evident in the modern world, especially, in the world of branding with some brands getting transformed & catapulted over time virtually to almost cult status and go on to develop almost a fanatic brand following, with the most prominent examples being Harley Davidson and the Volkswagen Beetle. However, charismatic leadership has to be grounded on the foundation & bedrock of ethics & morality to ensure that it does not deviate like a kamikaze on to the path of self-destruction.

However, deeper, subsequent modern probes into charisma have traced its roots to the realm of emotions and in fact intense, focused emotion which shows up in the body language first and then in the actual message. Charismatic leaders are simply authentic and thus, invariably have a perfect alignment between their body language and their message to the followers, thereby, producing charisma.[67, 68] Another related but different and more holistic concept is 'leadership presence' based on the "Three Levels of Leadership Model" developed by James Scouller and published in his titular book in 2011.

Charisma vs. Presence

Presence, contrastingly, also includes the leader's psychology, degree of personal self-mastery, authenticity and an attitude of service towards followers as the core tenets. Scouller has differentiated effectively between Charisma and Presence and has argued that "leaders can be charismatic by relying on a job title, fame, skillful acting or by the projection of an aura of "specialness" by followers – whereas presence is something deeper, more authentic, more fundamental and more powerful and does not depend on social status"[69].

Scouller has further defined Presence as follows, "At its root, it is wholeness – the rare but attainable inner alignment of self-identity, purpose and feelings that eventually leads to freedom from fear. It reveals itself as the magnetic, radiating effect you have on others when you're being the authentic you, giving them your full respect and attention, speaking honestly and letting your unique character traits flow. As leaders, we must be technically competent to gain others' respect, but it's our unique genuine presence that inspires people and prompts them to trust us – in short, to want us as their leader."[69] The two, however, are not mutually exclusive as there have been exceptional leaders who have exercised both charisma as

34

well as presence in an integrative manner.

Charismatic leadership evolved into one of the traditional theories of leadership of the yore having spilled over from its Sociology roots to Political Science & Management literature. Charismatic leadership focused on the personal characteristics as well as traits of the leader despite Weber having originally referred to the relationship between the leader and the followers as its core pivot.

In the Military sphere, the notions of charisma, presence & transformational leadership have traditionally been very well entrenched while holding their positions unrelentingly through the changing nature of warfare over the centuries. The following famous quote from the 34th U.S. President & the Supreme Commander of the Allied Forces during World War II, General Dwight D. Eisenhower, captured the essence of transformational leadership subtly with his following quote, 'Leadership is the art of getting someone else to do something you want done because he wants to do it'.

The key difference between traditional management purists and their military counterparts concerning authority & leadership is that while the former mostly & traditionally viewed the phenomenon from the transactional perspective with focus on performance-rewards based linear relationship, another perfect recipe for mediocrity, while the latter has traditionally focused on it from the Leader-Follower relationship, with a transformational perspective, duly focused on the unit/team and the mission.

Transformational Leadership

When a leader inspires his team members, who have full trust & confidence in him and are eager to go the extra mile in order to get the team over the line, rather than simply complying, it becomes transformational leadership in the verbiage of leadership theorists[15].

It is the leader's authenticity, connect & emotional conversation with the followers that produces charisma[65] with speeches by Winston Churchill during World War II and Martin Luther King, Jr. in the 1950s & 60s, during the American Civil Rights Movement, being prime examples. Similarly, Steve Jobs of Apple could be termed as the epitome of a charismatic business leader.

However, the leader does not necessarily need to possess charisma to exercise transformational leadership effectively as the military has shown by producing great leaders, as a process, over the centuries and the concept of leadership presence has shown.

The concept of Transforming leadership was first referred to by James MacGregor Burns in 1978 who took the concept of leadership beyond its traditional roots anchored in the transactional approach. He described it as a "process in which leaders & followers help each other to advance to a higher level of morale & motivation"[17].

Bernard M. Bass[18] evolved it into 'Transformational Leadership' by taking the concept a step further and elaborating it based on underlying psychological mechanisms at play. He explains that "transformation is at play when a transformational leader inspires & elevates his followers to go beyond their own self-interests to work towards the collective good and the team's success based on a mutually shared vision."[18] The leader with

36

charisma develops a personal, special emotional connect with his followers based on individualized consideration[18] by addressing their respective individual concerns & needs through coaching & mentoring etc.

Further, with his idealized influence, he inspires & stirs them up emotionally to take up challenges and go way above & beyond the line of duty for the team & the mission. The transformational leader, thus, gains respect & trust, instills a sense of pride in the team & leads as a role model with the followers looking up to him for inspiration with faith, respect & confidence. He gives them purpose, meaningful & challenging goals and in a way addresses their self-expression & self-actualization need, as outlined in the Maslow's hierarchy of needs theory of motivation.

How Transformational Leadership Works

Neuroscience says that human brains have an active goal seeking system or mechanism; as mentioned in the classic bestselling book Psycho-Cybernetics by Dr. Maxwell Maltz and also mentioned in Affective Neuroscience by Jaak Panksepp; which creates natural impulses to seek & chase meaningful & purposeful challenges. When a human being follows this urge to take on a purposeful, meaningful challenge, a neurotransmitter called Dopamine is released[30] by the brain making the person feel happy & motivated as this neurotransmitter is linked directly to motivation & pleasure. Once this process is repeated multiple times, it becomes a habit with the goal seeking mechanism within us getting fully activated. That's why it is said (originally by William Shakespeare) that adversity brings out the best in us. That's what life's battles have done to us humans by constantly challenging & prodding us which effectively made us move out of the cave to ultimately be able to land on the Moon and now head for Mars in the 21st century.

37

Transformational leadership has been the traditional backbone of military leadership as the team collectively faces high stakes, extraordinary situations, involving precious human lives, on a daily basis. A wrong call, in what are literally life & death situations, could seal the fate of many in a matter of minutes & seconds. That's what has driven soldiers to even dive over enemy grenades in combat zones in order to save their comrades from a certain death and not letting them & the team down come what may. There have been countless stories, transcending the borders of time and space, of extraordinarily brave soldiers staking & even losing their lives for their mates and for a cause larger than them.

The following short but highly inspirational speech given by Nike's founder Phil Knight in 1972; who dabbled in the shoe business as a fresher right out of college with $50 loaned from his father; reflects this transformational leadership effectively at work. He said to his employees, when Nike was going independent by breaking away from its Japanese partner, as elaborated brilliantly by him in his personal memoir, ShoeDog, "This is the moment we've been waiting for. Our moment. No more selling someone else's brand. No more working for someone else. Onitsuka has been holding us down for years. Their late deliveries, their mixed-up orders, their refusal to hear and implement our design ideas—who among us isn't sick of dealing with all that? It's time we faced facts: If we're going to succeed, or fail, we should do so on our own terms, with our own ideas— our own brand. We posted two million in sales last year . . . none of which had anything to do with Onitsuka. That number was a testament to our ingenuity and hard work. Let's not look at this as a crisis. Let's look at this as our liberation. Our Independence Day. Yes, it's going to be rough. I won't lie to you. We're definitely going to war, people. But we know the terrain. We know our way around Japan now. And that's one reason I feel in my heart this is a war we can win. And if we win it, when we win it, I see great things for us on the other side."[79]

Cricket, MSD & Transformational Leadership

K.L. Rahul recently unraveled as to what's behind MSD's greatness as a leader in an interview with YouTuber Ranveer Allahbadia, better known as 'Beer Biceps', following his getting injured in the middle of IPL 2023. K.L said, "MS Dhoni was my first captain. I've seen how he has handled the team, the calmness and the things that he does behind the scenes. Building the relationship with each person is something I've learnt from him. You need to build a relationship where these boys will fight for you, and with you. He has ways of building a relationship with each person. The bond that he creates... he has his own way. And he will know what's happening with each individual, personally and in his game. He knows everything about everybody, and that's what made him such a great leader". He further added, "I've realized much later, once when he retired and now he's not part of dressing room, I realized the presence of that man and the greatness that was a part of him."[102]

On the cricket field, this kind of leadership is what makes a player like Ravindra Jadeja go ballistic in the last over of an IPL match to score 37 runs off it and in the process take his team from an ordinary to an extraordinary position with an above-par score and effectively snapping up the match away from the opposition with the skipper MSD standing at the non-striker's end in an unusual turn of events, happy to play second fiddle to his partner. This magic of MSD-Jadeja duo has often been visible on the cricket field with Jadeja very often weaving the spin web and guiding his projectiles based on MSD's laser-based guidance system.

We have seen this in Virat Kohli's batting also quite often, especially in his pre-captaincy years, with him spearheading the Indian batting machinery as the core pivot to chase huge targets effortlessly for the team with an almost military-style discipline & commitment while playing down the ground through his innings and not playing any impulsive aerial shots to take the team to victory.

One particular inning, which has undoubtedly been one of his best innings & almost a crown jewel of his batting career and simply fails to fade away from the memory when one thinks of Kohli's batting, was played against Sri Lanka in the Commonwealth Bank Series played in Australia. It was a tri-series involving India, Australia and Sri Lanka and was part of India's horrendous tour down under during the 2011-12's season.

The India vs. Sri Lanka match was played on February 28, 2012 at the Bellerive, Oval in Hobart, Australia and it was a must-won game for India, in a two-horse race to be able to at least have a chance of qualifying for the final against Australia. Winning the game still couldn't have given a sure shot ticket to the final. It was a typical strategic situation in which the outcome just didn't simply depend on India's win or loss against Sri Lanka but also hinged on Sri Lanka's performance in their last match against the Aussies.

India won the toss and elected to field first, on a ground on which the average score batting first had been 300 in 2012, with the stats indicating an even, 50:50 split for wins between teams batting first vs. those batting second. Sri Lanka; powered by the exploits of Sangakkara & Dilshan, both of whom made centuries; put up a total of 320 for 4 in 50 overs. However, India were to get to 321 in 40 overs, in order to have any chance of staying alive in the tri-series based on net run-rate.

India lost the opening pair of Tendulkar & Sehwag in under 10 overs with the score being 86/2 in the tenth over with Gautam Gambhir and Virat Kohli taking on the mantle. Gambhir played his usual, run a ball game, making 63 of 64 balls before getting run out. Kohli, however, entrenched himself at the other end and put up an outstanding display of batting blitzkrieg at its best. The brilliant inning had clear shades of and definitely made one reminisce the nostalgic memories of Sachin's blasting of the Aussies under the Operation Desert Storm which had unleashed its fury on Sharjah in 1998. Kohli made 133 runs off just 86 balls which included 16 fours and 2 massive sixes. One of the best sixes ever from Virat came-off one of Malinga's attempted Yorker which went straight into the stands on the on-side somewhere between deep mid-wicket & deep square leg. His stand & deliver approach in one his best innings ever put the Lankans on the defensive and got India home in just 36.4 overs with the loss of 3 wickets and 80 balls still spare.

Virat was adjudged the Player of the Match and in the post match presentation he echoed the same feeling while terming it one of his best innings, "To be able to chase 320 in 40 overs in a must win game, and put that sort of a batting effort together was a great team effort. I committed a few mistakes in the last games after getting to 20 and 30, trying to middle every ball, which doesn't happen always in international cricket. This shows our character as a team, and how well we can execute our plans. It is about working hard and sticking in there. This is a special feeling, probably my best one-day innings so far."[16]

The leader of the pack, MSD, too was awestruck post the spectacular display of pyrotechnics, "This was some of the best ODI cricket I have been a part of. When you need 321 off 40, you need a good start. You need the quantity, but the quality ... We wanted to keep them down to 250, maximum 270.. We knew we had the firepower, but still 320 was more than we could digest. But once we got that start, we knew we could kick on"[16].

This is exactly what had happened at the Eden Gardens in 2001 under Dada's inspirational leadership; with the high pressure scenario and the match & the series on-the-line; catalyzing VVS's metamorphosis into Very Very Special Laxman that fateful day with that very special inning of 281, as the Aussies chose to remember him with the special moniker, while also transforming Rahul Dravid into the unforgettable 'The Wall'.

Why Transformational Leadership Works

What the leader also does in transformational leadership is that he instills a sense of pride, honour & belongingness to the team/unit in every member with the individual identities coalesced perfectly with the collective team identity and the team's cause placed way above & beyond any or every individual team member.

This collective identity drives the team to get the results harnessing the power of, what in the goal-setting theory's parlance is called, the superordinate goal, to full effect. That's what Virat Kohli and Ravindra Jadeja did on the two occasions mentioned above. This is what drove Dhoni & company in the T20 World Cup of 2007 (as redemption for the poor showing in the ODI World Cup of 2007 itself) & the ODI World Cup of 2011 to rise to the occasion and play for the country which elevated their game to an altogether new level and earned them the right to truly call themselves the undisputed World Champions. However, in 2011, the superordinate goal which the team seemingly had been working towards was to give a befitting farewell to the legend, Sachin Tendulkar, with the World Cup itself as the souvenir.

Gary Kirsten had following to say about Dhoni which succinctly explains his tremendous ability to execute Transformational Leadership effortlessly. Kirsten had said the following at the end of his 3 year tenure as the coach of Indian team. He said, "One word that comes to my mind about Dhoni's leadership is presence. I put the words — inspiration and presence — together, because I believe, I was in a position to inspire people through my work ethic whereas Dhoni was a leader for them through presence. He has this X-factor and walks around with his presence."[65] He further added, "Winning and losing don't mean a lot to him, he just gets on with it. He has this uncanny presence about him without saying much. People want to follow him, people want to go with him"[65].

He finished it with a statement that speaks volumes about Dhoni's leadership as well as their relationship and has also become one of his very famous quotes, "I want to go to war with this guy."[65]

Transformational Leadership and the Business World

This is what Kelly Johnson also did by creating Skunk Works in the late World War II years in 1943 as an advanced R&D unit housing the best of the best and almost handpicked aerospace designers & engineers. It was & has been much like the Top Gun of aerospace engineering which during the war years in the early 1940s started operations in a rented circus tent. The team had a unique identity (Skunks), special set of ground rules & practices and a high performance, challenge-oriented engineering culture along with an unconventional organizational approach which enhanced efficiency manifold. The team at Skunk Works never worked in silos and the word impossible did not exist in their lexicon with every complex technical challenge surmounted & overcome every time without compromising on safety, performance or quality.

The place was completely devoid of even the traces of red-tapism and bureaucracy as Kelly firmly believed that "they stifled innovation & hindered progress"[22]. The culture valued performance, ethics & quality output on time over everything else. That's how the Skunks developed & delivered multiple flying technological marvels, with some of them being outright technology miracles, during the second half of the Twentieth century, and effectively kept the world out of the clutches of World War III…

Learning Principle:

Transformational leadership works by instilling a sense of pride, honour & belongingness in each team member towards the team with the individual identities coalesced perfectly with the collective team identity and the team's cause placed way above & beyond any or every individual team member. This collective identity drives the team to get the results with each team member eager to go way above and beyond the call of duty while overcoming any & every obstacle in the way.

Chapter - III

DECENTRALIZED, SELF-DIRECTED TEAMS – THE INNER COMPASS AS THE GPS

Transformational Leadership and Self-Directed Teams

When a leader exercises Transformational Leadership, what he creates in the process, is a culture of high performance, strong goal-orientation & purpose-driven achievement and extreme ownership at the individual as well as collective level. This further creates highly motivated, skilled and self-directed teams capable of operating autonomously to take on any mission or task either with or without the leader. They are based on the decentralized organization principle and are also called self-directed teams working along a set of pre-defined objectives autonomously. In these specialized teams, the traditional hierarchy based command structures give way to flat, collaborative approaches which provide tremendous operational flexibility, resourcefulness & contingencies to navigate through murky waters & dark zones entailing unpredictable courses, uncertainty &

45

potentially hazardous situations. This operating model, thus, is very common in Special Operations Forces (SOF).

In the military lexicon, Special Operations Forces (SOF) units are the most prominent example & hallmark of self-directed teams with the term 'Special' innately drilled into the very core of their being. They go about their business under small teams-based structure & operating model, while leveraging their highly specialized training, capabilities, equipment and culture to the hilt, to achieve some of the toughest missions on earth while operating right below the enemy radar.

What typically differentiates the special-forces units & sets them apart from their conventional military counterparts effectively are their 'team first' attitude, unique culture and exhaustive training & operating standards which makes them the best of the very best. The amount of live ammunition typically consumed by a typical SEAL unit for training in just a couple of months is what a double sized Marine unit would exhaust in around a year and that is what sets the SEALs apart effectively. The U.S. Navy SEALs, operating under their coveted Trident insignia, have been the epitome of excellence and are some of the very best in their business. In the Indian context, Indian Navy's MARCOS and the National Security Guards (NSG) belong to that extraordinary & elite league of warriors.

Walking down the business corridors, the U.S. sporting goods giant, Nike's initial organizational culture and operating style, during its early days as a start-up, very much resembled & embodied the concept of self-directed teams comprising self-starters all the way who, operating like independent entrepreneurs, could be tactical as well as strategic simultaneously. The same has been elaborated extensively by Nike's founder Phil Knight in his personal memoir, titled, Shoe Dog[19] (more on it later).

On the cricket field, Indian cricket's transformational journey towards excellence started under Dada and reached its zenith under MSD with the process incrementally improved upon by others along the way despite occasional derailments, taking it off-the-track, caused by either internal or external disruptions. However, when a team continuously & constantly seeks improvement & perfection, after a while it becomes an innate part of the team culture, a sub-conscious habit at the individual as well as collective level, something which also alters the team DNA in the process, programming it for an eternal quest for improvement & success. After all, success breeds success.

The same was ratified in a study conducted by the Stony Brook University conducted in 2014 which found that, "early success bestowed on individuals produced significant increases in subsequent rates of success. The findings suggest that early success that is not based on merit may produce inequality in achievement among similarly qualified individuals. But the study also found that greater amounts of initial success failed to produce greater subsequent success." [93]

MSD, Transformational Leadership and Self-Directed Teams

When a team continuously & constantly seeks improvement & perfection, after a while it becomes an innate part of the team culture, a sub-conscious habit at the individual as well as collective level, something which also alters the team DNA in the process, programming it for an eternal quest for improvement & success. After all, success breeds success.

MSD echoed the same while elaborating in a candid media interview given to ESPN Cricinfo just 6 months after winning the T20 world cup in 2007 as to how winning that cup propelled the team on to the pathway &

habit of winning. He said, "In the Twenty20 World Cup we were thirsty. We tasted victory and we knew how it feels to be victorious. That really worked for us. The World Twenty20 win was the starting point - not from the victory point of view but the way we performed, the way we enjoyed each other's success. Even some of the senior guys who'd missed out, their involvement was great. Everybody was coming up with ideas; everybody wanted to win each and every game. That was the turning point. After that we started enjoying each other's success. If I score a hundred, of course I will enjoy it. But if your team-mates start enjoying your hundred that's when you know you are moving in the right direction. That's what is needed"[32].

The initial set of successes further build up temperament where the players and the team do not feel jittery and play with intensity while fully enjoying the game without pressure of expectations or outcome as failure is a perfectly acceptable part of the process but flinching & shirking away from giving one's hundred percent always under all circumstances is not. Winning becomes a habit and comes naturally to everyone at the conscious as well as sub-conscious level and even the big matches as well as tournament finals seem devoid of pressure & any major variation in mercury levels.

That's what's behind MSD's usual stoic, Spartan way of celebrating even after winning major tournaments combined with his minimalistic personal approach to degree of expression. However, that does not mean, as a corollary, that Ravindra Jadeja's grand swordplay with the bat upon reaching his 50s or Virat Kohli's in-the-face emotions on-field proves otherwise. MSD might have retired from international cricket but that winning & performance culture & DNA remains intact under the next set of players & leaders as shown by the team on their latest tour of Australia earlier this year.

Indian cricket has been on that long journey, geared towards an incessant pursuit of excellence, since the dawn of the twenty first century, as proved by the team's consistent upward movement & trajectory, assessed on the parameters of won/played percentage & win/loss ratio under different captains over the years, which shows a clear sign of a self-directed, winning team on the roll, barring the external disruption, which came in form of the appointment of an out of tune & culturally misfit coach over the 2005-2007 period.

Further evidence to that is visible on-field when one views the scenes of senior Indian players, usually, MSD, Virat & Rohit, engaging in collective decision-making by gathering at critical junctures of games to take tactical calls, which is a self-directed team's think tank holding a quick brainstorming session right in the middle of the battlefield to home-in on to a decisive course of action or to troubleshoot problems. In Dada's era, the members of this think tank used to be the Big 4, as they were called, comprising Sachin Tendulkar, Rahul Dravid, VVS Laxman and Dada himself.

Business World and Self Directed Teams

Two serial entrepreneurs, Ori Brafman and Rod Beckstrom, wrote a book titled, 'The Starfish and the Spider: The Limitless Power of Leaderless Organizations', exploring a major surge in the emergence of decentralized organizations in the business world in the internet age. They have opined in the book that, "Centralized organizations are like spiders and if the spider loses its head or legs the body just can't survive and will die. On the contrary, the decentralized & hybrid organizations are like the Starfish which have a flat structure with organs distributed through the body. The

Starfish, thus, has the remarkable ability to re-grow its lost limbs, unlike, the spider."[20]

A similar, decentralized philosophy is being applied in the development of electric flying crafts to be used as passenger-carrying flying taxis for congested urban cities, under the rapidly emerging concept of Urban Aerial Mobility (UAM) by Uber, and a horde of other industry players across most parts of the world. These flying crafts would feature Distributed Electric Propulsion (DEP) systems with multiple rotors & ducted propulsors powering the craft, thereby, adding a further safety element by effectively building in system redundancies (based on Murphy's Law) and booting out the possibility of a single point of failure from the equation.

This simply means that if one of the rotors fails mid-flight, the craft will not nosedive and will not come crashing down to the ground. By the way, system redundancy has been & remains the bedrock of safety in Aviation & Aerospace, based on the Murphy's Law, which states that anything that can go wrong with a system will eventually go wrong.

Nike also had this culture of self-starters and go-getter visionaries. A famous Harvard professor (who studied Nike in the 1970s) concluded in the end and told Phil Knight that, "Normally, if one manager at a company can think tactically and strategically, that company has a good future. But boy are you lucky: More than half the team (referring to Core Leadership group of Nike) think that way!"[79, 19]

It's the Self-Directed Teams that actually Run the Skunk Works

Going back to the Skunks, as they are popularly called, they were working on the development of the America's top secret; F-117 Night Hawk stealth aircraft program; way back in the late 1970s under Ben Rich's leadership. The program involved application of ground-breaking stealth technology which posed complex & multiple unprecedented engineering challenges which were to be addressed & resolved in time to meet the tight deadline of the F-117's maiden test flight to be conducted on December 1st of 1977.

During that phase, there was a worker's union strike staged at the Lockheed Corporation's plant in Burbank, California. This would surely have caused disruption as the project was awaiting final assembly of the first two prototypes and needed production workers for assembly. The strike was going to derail the project from its original, scheduled timelines for sure but one of the veteran shop superintendent, Bob Murphy, decided otherwise as it was a matter of pride for the stubborn Skunk Works.

Taking things in his own hands, while taking complete ownership, he assembled a team of engineers & managers for the final assembly of the two prototypes. Ben has written that "the team slogged 12 hours a day, 7 days a week for two long, consecutive months and assembled the prototypes on schedule without letting the timeline slip even by a wink"[13] and the F-117 Nighthawk took-off exactly on December 01, 1977.

That's the power of a self-directed team working with extreme ownership in action...

Learning Principle

Self-Directed teams are built & configured upon stability, experience and well-defined roles for members as the structural basis and autonomy, operational flexibility, resourcefulness & contingencies as the operating basis. They are given the broad mission objectives to be achieved rather than being provided the detailed tactical plan to be followed at every step of the process as they use their internal compass as the GPS for guidance. The infamous German Panzer Divisions during World War II operated as armored self-directed teams with a decentralized chain of command and owed much of their successes during the war to it. CSK that way is a highly self-directed IPL team given that every team member knows his role in the team very well and goes out on to the field to execute the same without any handholding by the team management. Even if one or few of the players get out the others can effectively take on the mantle to take the team across the finish line on any given day. That is why the typical team meetings at CSK under MSD do not last for more than a couple of minutes.

Chapter - IV

DOMAIN LEADERSHIP & PLAY-BY-WIRE – BEING AT THE ABSOLUTE TOP OF ONE'S GAME

Kelly was born in the remote mining town of Ishpeming, Michigan and grew up in a poor family which had emigrated from the city of Malmö, county of Scania, Sweden to the U.S. However, he had very strong interest in airplanes. He wanted to design & develop airplanes and made his first aircraft design sketch and even gave a short presentation about airplanes to neighbors & people of the surrounding area at a town hall at the age of 12. He slogged through his growing-up years to support the family. His mother used to wash & iron clothes of the neighboring community folks to generate additional sum for sustenance and Kelly had to deliver the clothes despite detesting the same to the core.

Kelly has written in his autobiography, "Kelly: More than My Fair Share of it All", that he used to take back streets to deliver the clothes to avoid being seen & teased by the children as always. However, one day, he got fed up & vowed to himself that, 'someday, he would take the best streets and not the back streets'[21] and would rise to prominence.

He had saved some amount by working alongside through his schooling years with which he wanted to learn flying and went to a pilot for the same. However, the pilot advised him, almost prophetically, to use that money wisely and rather go for university education by enrolling himself into a higher education program pertaining to aeronautics and Kelly did just that. He completed his bachelors & masters in aeronautical engineering from the University of Michigan.

At the university, he along with a friend decided & got permission to run the aeronautics department's wind tunnel over the weekends to earn some bucks to meet personal overhead expenses. That was the second half of 1920s and the airplanes as well as the race cars of the era didn't have aerodynamically efficient designs to be able to reduce drag. They did extensive wind tunnel testing for airplane & auto-makers apart from race car teams in the area to enhance aerodynamic efficiency of designs and actual race cars. This hard work & extensive experience with wind-tunnels would prove to be pivotal in his career later.

Lockheed Corporation had been developing its newest airliner, christened Model 10 Electra, in the 1932 which was to incorporate multiple technological leaps generationally. The Lockheed executives sought the opinion of Kelly's professor at the department of aeronautics at the University of Michigan regarding design stability. The design featured a single tail and the professor was convinced with the same. A precocious Kelly, however, studying in the final year by now, had major doubts about the directional stability with the single tail design based on his extensive operating experience with the wind tunnel by now.

He joined Lockheed Corporation as a tool designer, right after college in 1933, and told the Chief Design Engineer about his doubts with the

Electra's single tail design. He was told to go back to the University to carry out further wind tunnel testing of Electra's design with a scale model. He carried out almost 70 tests[23] in the wind tunnel and concluded that the single tail design lacked stability and a twin-tail design, on the contrary, would provide much more aerodynamic stability.

The twin-tale design was ultimately adopted by Lockheed and eventually became Lockheed's signature 'H-tail' which was used on a number of new aircrafts after that[23] as well. Electra proved itself to be a success which deservingly got Kelly the position of aeronautical engineer. His Chief Design Engineer, Hall Hibbard, said to Ben Rich years later, "That damn Swede, can actually see air"[21].

By 1938, Europe was on the verge of World War II with the continent getting deeper into the clutches of Hitler & his fellow Nazis. Lockheed Corporation was contacted by the U.K.'s Defense Ministry for the development of a maritime patrol aircraft cum light bomber for the Royal Air Force (RAF). A Lockheed team, including Kelly, left for Great Britain and proposed a variant of the Lockheed 14 Super Electra passenger airliner, which was Model 10 Electra's elder cousin. Based on British requirements, Kelly completely revamped the design of Lockheed 14 converting it from a passenger airliner into a coastal reconnaissance & light bomber aircraft in less than 72 hours using just his slide rules in a hotel room in England.

The design became the Royal Navy's A-29 Hudson with the British ordering almost 3,000 aircrafts from Lockheed through the Second World War which was the first major aircraft order for Lockheed and turned things around for the company which had just been pulled out of the bankruptcy under a new owner. He also designed the P-38 Lightning for the U.S. Air Force during the World War II and almost 10,000 P-38s were built.

By the 1950s, Kelly had become an industry authority on aviation and had become the Vice President of Advanced Development Projects (ADP), and the head of Skunk Works. Ben Rich has mentioned in his memoir, referring to the mid-1950s when the Skunks were working on the development of the U2, "I had never known anyone so expert at every aspect of airplane design & building. He was so sharp & instinctive that he often took my breath away."[13] He further adds, "I'd say to him, "Kelly," the shock wave coming off this spike will hit the tail". He would nod. "Yeah, the temperature there will be 600 degrees". I'd go back to my desk and spend two hours with a calculator and come up with a figure of 614 degrees."[13] That was the magic & genius of Kelly at its very best.

Kelly was simply born to be an airplane designer & engineer and was just extraordinary at that. He himself said years later, "I knew I wanted to design airplanes since I was twelve years old,"[24]

The SR-71 Blackbird, the fastest manned, air-breathing flying machine in the world ever built, was developed in the early 1960s under Kelly as his magnum opus and still holds the record of being the fastest in the world, with an astonishing top speed of Mach 3.2+, which translates into almost 3,000 feet per second or almost a Kilometer per second and 3,600 KMs per hour; which is the equivalent of covering the lengths of 3 football fields in the quantum of time it takes for a person to sneeze or pick up something from the floor while flying at an altitude of 80,000 feet almost at the edge of space.

During its in-service career, which spanned from early 1960s to the 1990, almost 100+ Surface to Air Missiles (SAMs) were fired at the

Blackbird but none of them could even come near it, forget about touching it and it remained unbeaten throughout its almost 3-decades long service career. The Soviet MiG fighter jets, too, could only fly up to an altitude of 65,000 feet and were no-match for the flying beast.

The Blackbird was simply 'Untouchable', as the 20-odd elite pilots flying it have put it and nothing could stop it or come in its way. Multiple USAF pilots have recounted & mentioned in their personal memoirs as to how they would hail Kelly & his fantastic creation every time the Blackbird would successfully outrun the incoming SAMs simply with its incredible speed to take them safely out of the harm's way, reliably on every single occasion.

It would fly with utter impunity, like a streaking meteor, at the top of the stratosphere, almost at the edge of the space where no manned machine could dare to soar & survive to tell the tale except the Blackbird. The incredible machine he and the Skunk Works team built was a pure technological miracle, was way ahead of its time and truly belonged to the 21st century while being produced in the 20th itself. That's domain leadership…from the perspective of the creator as well as the creation.

The secrets to his genius & outstanding career success, however, were anchored in an eternal passion for airplanes coupled with extreme hard work & grit, especially, the years slogged in the University's wind tunnel which gave him the extraordinary vision to 'see air' while also giving him an edge over others at the very outset of his career.

The nuances & extreme challenges of high altitude flying were learnt by Kelly early in his career at Lockheed while working with Wiley Post, the famous & ingenious American pilot, who became the first man to fly solo around the world in 8+ days in his Lockheed Vega aircraft in 1931, which he had bought in 1926 with the settlement money received as compensation for an oil field accident in which he had lost his left eye. Post was also the first man to discover jet stream and developed one of the world's first high altitude pressure suits as well.

The development of SR-71 Blackbird, too, entailed monumental engineering challenges as every single, traditional process of airplane development & production had to be reinvented from scratch. The inexorable process started with the special tools which had to be developed from scratch for working with Titanium to the special fuel, with a very high flash point, which had to be developed especially for the Blackbird to fly with, as elaborated vividly by Kelly in his autobiography. Kelly & Skunks grappled with, addressed & surmounted every single engineering problem simply with their adroitness, ingenuity & determination and were ready with the first Blackbird in flat 20-months from contract award. The G in Genius, thus, invariably stands for Grit…

Even, psychology has sworn by the power of grit. Psychologist, Angela Duckworth, has mentioned in her bestselling book, "Grit: The Power of Passion & Perseverance", that the "Secret to outstanding achievement is not talent but a special blend of passion and persistence she calls "grit." Angela has found that grit—a combination of passion and perseverance for a singularly important goal—is the hallmark of high achievers in every domain."[25]

MSD & Domain Leadership

Coming to MSD; interestingly, MSD's personal, growing up story has remarkable similarities with Kelly's early life story. Even MSD had very humble beginnings and was born in a family of inter-state migrants who had moved to Ranchi, Jharkhand in 1964 from their native village in Almora, Uttarakhand. His father was a pump operator working with a public sector engineering firm, MECON Ltd. and he grew up in a room-house measuring a mere eighty square feet in size[26].

MSD also showed remarkable grit in paving his own runway for take-off & then charting his course from Ranchi to the highest echelon of Indian cricket while taking a railroad detour in between and battling tremendous odds all the way to make his way to the very top of the game. In the process, he turned & transformed himself effectively into an entirely different class of composite baked under the searing heat of the pressures, odds & challenges he faced & successfully surmounted.

This way, he developed extraordinary skills & capabilities as an explosive batsman and a great captain with immense firepower, unconventional shots and nerves of titanium which could stay cool & mission-focused even in the heat of the moment. This outstanding structural ability to withstand enormous heat & pressure propelled him on-course to eventually become the Indian cricket's 'Captain Cool'.

What he also developed, along the way, has been an almost superhuman, holistic cricketing sense & brilliant brainpower bandwidth & processing capacity ranging wide across & encompassing all aspects of the game from the strategy as well as the tactical perspective. This became a definite edge for the team over opponents and has proved to be decisive on multiple occasions.

Domain leadership, in contrast from the traditional connotation of leadership, i.e. people leadership, stands for specialists who have expertise in a particular domain. They use that domain authority to influence & help others, for anything across the board, having to do with that domain. One of the most prominent example of MSD's on-field cricketing prowess has been the unofficial rechristening of the Decision Review System (DRS) to the Dhoni Review System (DRS) by the media commentators, viewers & fans given the extraordinarily high degree of statistical accuracy, validity & reliability of his calls to take the DRS or not which very often has proved to be decisive for India by tilting the scales of the game in India's favour on multiple occasions at critical junctures of the game. Thus, this domain leadership enables the leader to tactically assess the situation extraordinarily and take the best call in the given, on-field scenario.

MSD had himself said in 2008 after the T20 world cup winning campaign, "Being a wicketkeeper really helped me more than anything. In India you have to make quite a few bowling changes, because at times when a partnership is going and the wicket is flat and you are playing with four bowlers, it gets tough for the skipper. That's the time you step in - being the keeper you read the wicket well. That really helped me more than anything else."[32] The experience of closely watching the game from behind the stumps, cricket's unique vantage point, in over hundreds of games undoubtedly has been the secret to his unusually high accuracy & success with DRS calls.

Another example was on display in the IPL 2021's CSK match played against Rajasthan Royals in which Dhoni helped Jadeja take the crucial wicket of the in-form Jos Buttler, who was spearheading RR's campaign to a potential victory with his explosive batting. Jadeja was called back into the attack to bowl by MSD when Buttler was playing on 49 and had hammered Jadeja earlier in the first two overs of his bowling. Buttler welcomed Jadeja by hitting Jaddu for a six right away with the ball getting dispatched deep into the stands & disappearing. The Umpires called for a similarly used ball as per the rule and the usual practice.

Dhoni told Jadeja, as captured by the stump mic, that since the ball is dry the next delivery is going to turn & grip, so ball accordingly. Jadeja was spot on & was not going to miss the opportunity. He bowled Buttler right through the gates at the score of 49 which led to RR losing subsequent wickets like a pack of cards & ultimately lost the match to CSK. It was MSD's immense experience, cricketing brain and presence of mind which enabled Jadeja and CSK to stage an effective comeback at a crucial stage in the game.

The 'Fingertip Feel' or 'Fingerspitzengefühl'

What these stalwarts of the domain tend to develop is a snap mental calculation or what is also called is a fingertip feel or 'Fingerspitzengefühl', in the German lexicon where it originated, with the term standing for 'intuitive flair' or 'instinct' or 'one's finger on the pulse'. Additionally, it also entails great situational awareness along with situational management with the ability to respond most appropriately & tactfully in a given situation. MSD, in fact, has talked very often about him being a pure instinct player & captain not believing & relying much on stats or theories.

The foremost example of the usage of the term has been in the context of World War II, and specifically, the German Army's elite & ingenious commander in the North African war theater, Erwin Rommel, who was duly given the nickname, the 'Desert Fox', by the tormented British forces. The war legend has it that Rommel had this uncanny ability or Fingerspitzengefühl to anticipate every move the British would conceptualize to attack him or his position and he would 'outfox' them every time on the nebulous desert terrain while also catching the enemy forces off-guard while attacking them with his wily tactical maneuvers and the Panzer Divisions.

Rommel himself has elaborated about his exploits as an unassuming tank commander in the battlefields of World War I, in his military classic & bestselling 1930s book, Infantry Attacks, which subsequently propelled his rise to the top echelons of the German Army as the Field Marshal Rommel. His battle tactics, maneuvers, campaigns & the unorthodox mind through the battles of World War II, as the 'Desert Fox', have been analyzed exquisitely by famous historian & the former U.S. Army Helicopter pilot, during the Vietnam War, Samuel W. Mitcham Jr., in his book, Desert Fox: The Storied Military Career of Erwin Rommel.

MSD and 'Fingerspitzengefühl'

This Fingerspitzengefühl is what guides MSD whether to take DRS calls or not in high pressure situations apart from the seemingly outlandish calls taken on the spur of the moment on multiple occasions, like giving the ball to Praveen Kumar in 2007's Twenty20 tournament's final or his decision to bat himself up the order in 2011's ODI World Cup final, both of which ultimately turned out his way. This could be called & termed, play-by-wire, and that's because analogously in aviation the fly-by-wire technology involves pilot's commands going to the on-board computers first and then getting relayed to the airplane's control surfaces for execution. It, thus, in turn, refers to MSD's onboard super computer being effectively at play.

Even MSD himself says that his gut feeling is based on his past & vast experience. In an interview given to bcci.tv given in 2014 he had said, "I don't plan a lot and believe in my gut feel. But what many people don't understand is that to have that gut feel, you have to have experienced that thing before. My gut feeling comes from my past experiences of all the cricket I've played in my life and the situations I have faced. It's not something you just feel for a moment without any logic."[84] He further elaborated the same with an example, he said, "For instance, you don't know anything about bikes. I open one of my bike engines and keep it in front of you and ask you 'which model does your gut feeling say this engine belongs to', you will be clueless. You won't have a gut feeling because you don't know anything about the object there."[84]

K.L. Rahul shared further about MSD's absolute belief in his gut feel and how he even told Rahul to trust it in a recent interview, "He said this to me a lot of times... trust your gut as a captain. That's something he did, as a leader and as a person in general. The first thought that you get, you always question it, but he never questioned it. If he had a gut feeling about a certain thing, he would never try to question it or second-guess it. He did it, whether it went well or didn't go well. That's what helped him in a lot of ways. That's why he was unorthodox in a lot of ways, people didn't understand at the time but he trusted his gut feeling. That's why he got results too."[102]

This remarkable ability of his to assess & read the game brilliantly also led to his ascent to the helm as the captain of the team. MSD recounted this in an interview while also unveiling about & ascribing the role Sachin Tendulkar played in it. He said, "It did (surprise me), because I was never really aiming for captaincy. I think it was more about the interactions that I had with them. For instance, whenever Sachin came on to bowl - and because he could bowl so many different deliveries - he would ask me what the best ball would be - seam-up, leg-spin, off-spin - depending on the wicket and the batsman. Perhaps the honest opinions I gave him at these points made him believe that I read the game well." [84]

Why Domain Leadership Works?

What these extraordinary achievers also bring with them in their respective domains is an unparalleled, natural authority & respect as leaders, which makes them clearly stand a class apart, like a lighthouse with the guiding beacon, which naturally brings respect to them in the leadership role. This is what has brought him respect even from the opposition players. As transformational leaders, they inspire & motivate their followers to consistently pursue excellence, outperform and go beyond their limitations while following & fulfilling their internal sense of purpose. They also help & enable their followers in consistently upping their game by a notch or two to a further higher orbit by guiding them with their experience & wisdom while providing the much needed directional course & nudge.

MSD has been a natural at mentoring & coaching young players as we all have seen over the years. For MSD, this list includes the bigwigs of India's present cricket line-up, including, Virat Kohli, Rohit Sharma, Ravindra Jadeja, Hardik Pandya and the spinning duo of Kuldeep & Chahal at some point or the other of their playing careers. Also, his mentoring & coaching initiatives have not just remained restricted to the men he commanded on-field in the national cricket team or the CSK. He has often been seen even mentoring young players from other teams in the IPLs as well.

A new entrant to the Indian women's cricket team, Indrani Roy, recently mentioned as to how MSD has helped her improve her game, especially, the wicket keeping part of it. She said, "During a training session in Ranchi sometime last year, I had a long conversation with Mahi Sir about how to improve my game and he had told me that I should ensure that I improve my reflexes and movement in the five-metre radius. For wicketkeepers, that's a key thing and he advised me that I should try and get better. That actually helped me."[27]

India's Chinaman spinner, Kuldeep Yadav, too, reminisced the guidance, he used to receive as a bowler from MSD entrenched behind the stumps. He said, "Sometimes I miss that guidance because he (Dhoni) has great experience. He used to guide us from behind the wickets, kept screaming. We miss his experience."[28]

Another Indian player, who has credited MSD for his rise as a premier, specialist power-play bowler in the T20 format has been Deepak Chahar. He recently said in a media interview to the Times of India, "It was a long-cherished dream of mine to play under Mahi bhai. I have learnt a lot under his captaincy. I have taken my game to another level under his guidance. He has always backed me. He taught me how to take responsibility. There is no one in my team (CSK) who bowls three overs in the powerplay. I do that. That's because of Mahi bhai. Bowling the first over for a team is not an easy job. With time, I have improved and learned how to control the flow of runs, especially in T20s."[29] He further added, "He (Dhoni) knows his players well and he uses them wisely. He knows who is good at the death, who is good in the power-play and who is good in the middle overs. I have been scolded by him a lot, but I know those talks and that guidance has benefitted me a lot as well and helped me grow as a bowler"[29].

Rohit Sharma, the Indian Hitman, also credits MSD for his career transformation with MSD's decision to send him up the batting order as an opener which effectively unlocked & paved the way to his phenomenal career success. He said in a media interview in early 2017 that "MSD's reading of a player's ability is peerless"[55]. He further added, "With no disrespect to other great Indian captains, I was blessed to play under MS all these years. His calmness in pressure situations helped us. He always led from the front. There won't be one like him."[55]

Even Yuvraj Singh echoed the same sentiment about MSD around the same time in early 2017. Yuvi said, "He was the best captain ever, I would like to tell you that and it's been amazing playing under you (talking to MSD), winning three big championships - winning the World Cup and being the No.1 Test team"[56].

The extraordinary domain competence, thus, enables the leader to mentor & shape his troops effectively while the special, personal connect he develops in the process lets him to marshal & inspire his troops to go above & beyond the call of duty on the battlefield and bridge that gap between the ordinary and the extraordinary.

However, there have also been leaders who have been an exception and have not really been domain experts in any sense of the term. However, they have proved to be equally effective with the most relevant example here being Apple's Steve Jobs. He was not an engineer or someone with a bright technical background. What he instead was is what is called a visionary. He himself said when Steve Wozniak asked him about what does he really do. Jobs said, "Musicians play their instruments. I play the orchestra". He was like the conductor of an orchestra which would go on to compose timeless & wonderful melodies. However, that was in the entrepreneurial context of business with a strategic leadership background against an organizational backdrop, wherein, what investors, as stakeholders, are really bothered about is the outcome & results, which are mostly financial in nature.

Learning Principle

Thus, in a small, high performance team set-up, organized to carry out a specialist mission in a specific domain, be it the Navy SEALs for Combat, the Skunks for Aerospace Engineering or a National Sports Team; it comes down to decisive tactical leadership, especially that play-by-wire, consisting of tactics or maneuvers, wherein, the team leader has to be one of the best in the game to lead the team to outmaneuver the challenges as well as the opponents and to get the team home successfully while leading by example all the way. The leader develops a special, personal connect with his team members which lets him marshal & inspire them to go above & beyond the call of duty and outperform.

Chapter V

HUMILITY & HUMBLE LEADERSHIP – THE ATTITUDE OF SERVING, SERVICE & CARE – THE HUMAN CONNECT

Humility etymologically originates from Latin, humilis, meaning low. Thus, the word humble comes to describe 'what is ranked somewhat low' by others in its literal meaning. The Merriam-Webster dictionary defines humility as, "the freedom from pride or arrogance", which also indicates the areas in which the humble person is low. Humility has strong correlation with wisdom & grace, which have been the traditional cornerstones of leadership, with humility also considered as the mother of all virtues.

Psychological research, in fact, has shown a very strong correlation between humility as a personality factor and a number of other qualities, including, sincerity, modesty, fairness, truthfulness and authenticity. Psychologists have in turn developed an extension of the Big 5 personality model with the addition of honesty-humility or the H-factor as the sixth dimension of personality, in the development of the HEXACO model, developed by Ashton & Lee and mentioned in their book, The H Factor of Personality.

Humble Leadership

The business & leadership literature has recently been imbued by the concept of humble leadership, as postulated by the father of organizational culture studies, Edgar Schein in his 2018 book, Humble Leadership: The Power of Relationships, Openness & Trust, wherein, he has outlined that instead of focusing on power-led leadership & control under the traditional top-down concept of leadership; which stokes insecurity & fear in the followers ultimately leading to loss of motivation; the leader's focus should be on service, led by humility, to bring out the best in his team.

The focus of the leader should not be on himself as the captain of the ship but rather on the followers with the relationships shaped by transparent communication, openness, trust & empathy; instead of hierarchy & power distance; the hallmarks of traditional & the conventional concept of leadership. Humility also enables the leader to focus on his own shortcomings and keep evolving as a person as well as the leader.

Why Humble Leadership Works

An article published on Forbes titled 'Why Humble Leaders make the Best Leaders', outlines further, "A number of research studies have concluded that humble leaders listen more effectively, inspire great teamwork and focus everyone (including themselves) on organizational goals better than leaders who don't score high on humility. At a managerial level, traits associated with humility—such as soliciting feedback and focusing employee needs—generated higher levels of engagement and job performance from their direct reports, according to research published in Administrative Science Quarterly. Humble leaders understand that they are not the smartest person in every room. Nor do they need to be. They encourage people to speak up, respect differences of opinion and champion the best ideas, regardless of whether they originate from a top executive or a production-line employee."[94]

Humble leaders, as leaders, thus, focus on the development of their followers as well, in the process, rather than treating them as just means to get to end results. This creates a culture of trust, openness, relationship, camaraderie & mutual respect shaped by transparent & open communication. This interpersonal culture of transparency & communication, in combination with the culture of extreme ownership, under a leader exercising transformational leadership, to inspire his team to chase challenging goals, leads to extraordinary results in myriad ways.

Humility and Business

Phil Knight's leadership style during Nike's early years when the company operated as a team of family & friends, as elaborated by him in Shoe Dog, epitomized it and was all about this.

Maruti Udyog Limited's Managing Director, late Mr. Jagdish Khattar, would ensure that he would have meals with the workers in the company's staff canteen regularly as he believed that it helped him break the traditional barriers of hierarchy and enabled him to effectively develop a strong connect with his people. He said in a media interview, "I eat with them. There is no better way to build bonds with them."[31] Another of his pet initiative was to provide unlimited meals to the workers so that they could eat as much as they wanted[31] geared towards building morale & motivation.

MSD & Humility – Synonymous with Each Other

MSD's take on humility as a person could simply be gauged from the following statement given by the security head of MECON Ltd., the company where Dhoni's father worked and which provided the accommodation where Dhoni spent his childhood years. He said to media, "Dhoni Sir still comes to this place whenever he passes from this area! That is the beauty of his humility as he has never forgotten his roots."[26]

On the professional front, one of Dhoni's statements, which came in an interview given to ESPN Cricinfo way back in March 2008, barely just six months after he had captained India to the Twenty20 World Cup win in 2007, remarkably echoed the core tenets of humble leadership. Dhoni had said, "More than being a successful captain, I've got a successful team who want go out there, who want to enjoy cricket, who want to give more than 100%. They take everything as a challenge, whether it's fielding, bowling, batting, off-the-field activities or anything. It's not about the captain, because once in a while you take a big decision that has a big impact. It's more about the individual - how they respond to you and what kind of relationship you have with your team"[32].

He again emphasized the point in 2014 with his statement, "For me, being a part of the team is much more important than being the captain."[84]

He further added, "I believe in giving a guy a consistent period to perform, not make him think, "If I'm not performing in this game or a few games, I won't be part of the team". I like taking all the guys into a comfort zone and creating the best atmosphere where they can perform. Till now I've been successful." [32] He, thus, clearly chose & effectively instilled the culture of performance & relationships rather than taking the traditional, power-led model of leadership which invariably leads to mediocrity, insecurity & fear while also stifling creativity.

In this context; a quote from Gary Kirsten, sheds further light on Dhoni's signature, 'Captain Cool' temperament. He said, "The admirable thing is that in the three years that I was with him, he never lost his temper even once. We operate in a highly volatile and emotional environment and you always knew from the leader that he was never going to lose his temper but you knew he meant business when he had something to say." [65]

Dhoni also jettisoned the pressure of expectations & outcomes from his ship which enabled his crew to express themselves, be creative, enjoy themselves in the field and innovate by clearly stating his expectations, as follows, "I believe in giving more than 100% on the field and I don't really worry about the result if there's great commitment on the field. That's victory for me." [32]

Another latest comment from Team India's opening batsman, K.L. Rahul, in an interview given to Forbes India, underscores MSD's humble journey & humility. Rahul said, "Something I have learned from him is how humble he has been through ups and downs, how he has put his country ahead of everything is just unbelievable" [101]

On the field, he believed in bringing out the best in his team by inspiring, motivating & challenging them to seek excellence and driving them along, with a strong personal connect, on the journey towards success. He said about this personal connect, "One of my theories is to be captain on the field and off the field you need to totally enjoy each other's company. I don't like discussing cricket off the field." [32] He further added, "If your dressing-room atmosphere is great then most of the time you'll get a favourable result. That was very important and I was actually marking it. He also stressed its importance for the new guys, "Especially guys who've not played at the international level - when they see a relaxed dressing room that's what stays in their mind."[32]

Authority vs. Influence

John C. Maxwell, author of the leadership classic, 'The 21 Irrefutable Laws of Leadership', says, "The true measure of leadership is influence, nothing more and nothing less."[33] Influence, thus, is way distinct from authority and the leader derives his influence to lead from caring for others instead of simply commanding others and that distinction is critical for the leader to understand. A leader, thus, cares about his relationships with his followers qualitatively and the impact his actions may have on the followers.

MSD's care about the safety & well-being of his team-mates was visible in the IPL 2021, with the tournament at the half-way juncture, when COVID-19 permeated into the CSK team with two positive cases reported. CSK refused to play their very next game against Rajasthan Royals owing to quarantine requirements of those exposed and also to ensure safety of the players. He was also the last one to leave the team hotel; when the tournament was ultimately scrapped days later; as the captain of the ship, wanting to ensure that everyone of his team members reached home safely before boarding his flight back home to Ranchi.

However, the important point here is that the leader has to be really genuine & authentic in his care towards his team rather than just feigning it else he can't cut it and everything just goes for a toss.

Also, MSD has probably been the only one to have gone out of the way to address & praise even the CSK's reserve players on the bench who hadn't got the opportunities to play. In one of the post match presentation, he said, "Last 8-10 years we've not changed lot of players so they know our approach. Also we appreciate the players not playing a lot. Only way you can put it forward is having those nice interactions. You might be feeling why a player is getting a lot chances, it's natural. But we tell them you too will get your chance. Just try to have the faith and frame of mind where if you get the opportunity you'll be ready. Keeping the dressing room atmosphere healthy is important. It's not an easy thing. When you're at the top level you want to play. Have to give extra credit to the players who've not played so far."[95] These are small measures which go a long way in boosting & bolstering overall team morale.

CSK's bowling coach & former Indian pacer, Lakshmipathy Balaji, feels that MSD fundamentally altered the perceptions of leadership & captaincy forever. Balaji said, while speaking on the Star Sports Tamil show 'Cricket Connected - Aatam Thodarattum' a year ago in 2020, "From the year 2000, according to me, there's nobody like Dhoni who's had such a massive influence on not just Indian cricket but world cricket. His leadership changed the perception of leadership among all captains. The way he maintains his emotion on field, maintaining the team environment and camaraderie, leading the team successfully, only MS Dhoni could do it."[85]

Humble Leadership in Military Context

In this context & aspect of leadership, the conduct of General Jim Mattis of the United Sates Marine Corps, who is also referred to as the 'Warrior Monk' and known by the nickname, 'Mad Dog', which has been more of a misnomer as he rarely lost his cool, was exemplary and worth mentioning here. Gen. Mattis has mentioned in his leadership book authored with Bing West, Call Sign Chaos: Learning to Lead, a incident which brings out the essence of the same. The following real story (an excerpt) was also narrated by General Krulak in a lecture[34] held at the Center for the Study of Professional Military Ethics at the U.S. Naval Academy:-

"General Krulak said, when he was Commandant of the Marine Corps, every year, starting about a week before Christmas, he and his wife would bake hundreds and hundreds and hundreds of Christmas cookies. They would package them in small bundles. Then on Christmas day, he would load his vehicle. At about 4 a.m., General Krulak would drive himself to every Marine guard post in the Washington-Annapolis-Baltimore area and deliver a small package of Christmas cookies to whatever Marines were pulling guard duty that day. He said that one year, he had gone down to Quantico as one of his stops to deliver Christmas cookies to the Marines on guard duty.

He went to the command center in Virginia and gave a package to the lance corporal who was on duty. He asked, "Who's the officer of the day?" The lance corporal said, "Sir, it's Brigadier General Mattis." And General Krulak said, "No, no, no. I know who General Mattis is. I mean, who's the officer of the day today, Christmas day?" The lance corporal, feeling a little anxious, said, "Sir, it is Brigadier General Mattis." General Krulak said that, about that time, he spotted in the back room a cot, or a daybed. He said, "No, Lance Corporal. Who slept in that bed last night?" The lance corporal said, "Sir, it was Brigadier General Mattis." About that time, General Krulak said that General Mattis came in, in a duty uniform with a sword, and General Krulak said, "Jim, what are you doing here on Christmas day? Why do you have duty?" General Mattis told him that the young officer who was scheduled to have duty on Christmas day had a family, and General Mattis decided it was better for the young officer to spend Christmas Day with his family, and so he chose to have duty on Christmas Day. General Krulak said, "That's the kind of officer that Jim Mattis is."

.   Gen. Mattis would always put his team's needs above his own. Another incident shared by Nate Fick, a former Marine Captain, in his book One Bullet Away, makes it crystal clear. He has written, while mentioning about his combat experiences under the command of Gen. Mattis while fighting across the battlefields of Afghanistan & Iraq, "No one would have questioned Mattis if he'd slept eight hours each night in a private room, to be woken each morning by an aide who ironed his uniforms and heated his MREs. But there he was, in the middle of the freezing night, out on the lines with his Marines."[36] The usage of 'his' by Nate explains it all here.

That's real leadership and the cult of Gen. Mattis…

Humble Leadership and the Indian Military History Context

In the Indian context, the leadership story that comes closest to it and has the distinction of being a cult of its very own has been of none other than the ruler of Mewar, Maharana Pratap and the forest dwelling tribal community of Bhils, who were well known for their prowess with arms. After losing the battle of Haldighati in 1576, in which Bhil archers fought for Mewar's army, Maharana Pratap stayed with his Bhils in the forests surrounding Mewar resiliently for years while trying to stage resurgence with the help of his Bhil army. While staying with the Bhils and living their austere lifestyle, he developed an intimate bond with them with the distinction between the leader and the followers evaporating & almost becoming indistinguishable.

The Bhils used to treat him like one of their very own and fought with guerrilla warfare tactics under him even at the cost of their lives to help him reclaim his kingdom which he ultimately did. The cultural & military history of Mewar kingdom still has a special place for the invaluable role & contribution of Bhils written in golden letters as well as spirit of the region and showcased prominently.

Maharana Pratap has been an eternal Indian legend and the story of his unique bond with his subjects and the incredible fight back spearheaded by the Bhil army simply stuff of legends & part of folklore for the generations…

On a final note, humble leaders, thus, may not have charisma or a powerful, commanding presence but their quiet presence, emotional intelligence and focus on, as well as care for others, simply leads to great outcomes for the organizations led by them. The same was unearthed by researcher & author, Jim Collins; who did a seminal, longitudinal research on successful companies looking to decrypt their mojo at work. He found irrefutable evidences of multiple organizations getting transformed from ordinary to great with humble leaders at the helm and subsequently authored the book, 'Good to Great', two decades back at the turn of the century, in which he propounded & elaborated the same.

Learning Principle – Leading by Care with the Human Connect

Humble leaders may not have the charisma or a powerful, commanding presence but their quiet presence, emotional intelligence and focus on, as well as care for their followers & others, makes them win their hearts and simply provides a significant influence over them which when exercised delivers great outcomes for the organizations led by them.

CHAPTER VI

SUPER-ORDINATE GOALS – HARNESSING THE INCREDIBLE POWER OF HUMAN EMOTIONS

'Super' etymologically means above the ordinary, from Latin 'Supra' meaning 'above, over or beyond'. Super-ordinate goals, thus, literally are goals which are above or beyond ordinary goals. Super-ordinate goals, in the verbiage of goal-setting, are goals which provide meaning & purpose to an individual, team or an organization by being their very raison d'etre. In the organizational context, super-ordinate goals are postulated in the Vision & Mission statements of an organization and are much different from the ordinary financial or performance goals. In the cricketing parlance, an example of a super-ordinate goal for an individual would be to take the team to victory rather than an ordinary goal of being the player of the match in that particular fixture with the former holding a much higher meaning & value proposition for a player than an individual feat on any given day.

In social psychology, super-ordinate goals are used to make groups at conflict to rather cooperate with each other by working together towards achievement of such goals which effectively leads to reduction in the intensity of their conflict.

Why Super Ordinate Goals Work?

How are these super-ordinate goals so effective and what is the mechanism by which they work? That's essentially the domain of neuroscience with the lead & pivotal role held by a neurotransmitter within our brain, known as Dopamine, as mentioned earlier as well. Dopamine, as an essential element of the brain's neurochemistry, performs a myriad of functions in the human body.

However, from the perspective of motivation & performance, what it does is make a situation, goal or task feel salient & meaningful to us[37] and provides the motivation to work towards achieving the same. It happens with the release of Dopamine into specific areas of our brains[38], which, in addition to providing motivation, essentially also signals feedback for predicted & anticipated rewards likely to come our way from the achievement of the goal and it does it as a mechanism.

Thus, for a player, from the neuroscience perspective, the goal of playing a match winning inning for the team to take it to victory is much more salient, meaningful & fulfilling for the brain than a selfish goal of making a century for himself and being named as the player of the match. That's how the human brain is wired and it works the same way for altruism & pro-social behavior, wherein, helping others provides a similar sense of joy & satisfaction. Also, it is not restricted to just humans with even animals showing elements of altruistic behavior. For instance, Dolphins have actually been reported to help other Dolphins stuck in the nets.[45], [46],

The Working Mechanism of Super Ordinate Goals

That's the phenomenon at work when we see Virat Kohli batting almost like a possessed man while chasing targets with the goal of getting team India to victory, especially in close or crucial matches. That is what also explains his incredible surge in batting averages while chasing targets, as against his career average, which literally goes into a super gear. Same goes for his batting average, which witnesses a major spike, while playing overseas as against home conditions.

The more challenging it is treated by the brain, greater the motivation & the drive to perform and achieve with the body & mind operating in tandem in the overdrive mode, almost like the afterburner mode of a fighter jet engine delivering a tremendous surge in thrust, speed, maneuverability & performance for the high-G dogfights. Virat, seemingly, has simply perfected & almost drilled the process into his very core with sheer grit & perseverance.

At this point, it is important to note that this is what Virat's process has been, unlike, MSD, whose process has pivoted around leading from behind the stumps as well as his teammates with leadership as the core tenet of his captaincy with the captain cool guiding & nudging them skillfully as the leader of the pack to ensure that they enjoy their game with him coming to the fore with the bat only when the team really required him.

Virat's process, on the contrary, has been about leading from the front with batting being the core of his captaincy (so far) supplemented by his aggressive tactics & on-field aggression. MSD, as the wicket-keeper captain, thus, has been the odd one out in the league of Indian captains who have mostly either been top or middle order batsmen with the other exception to the trend being the great Kapil Dev himself.

Dopamine's activation of reward pathways in the brain has also been associated with a role in addiction, as per the scientists. Thus, when we achieve our goals and feel that rush of dopamine we start wanting it more often and almost craving for it neurologically. When we start chasing challenging goals this way often it becomes a habit and success becomes almost an addiction. This is not a new phenomenon.

However, it happens almost at the sub-conscious level for everyone occasionally and most of us are not even aware of this at the conscious level. But, when this phenomenon or the brain mechanism is leveraged upon consciously, it leads to us being able to control as to when, where & how to make it kick into action, almost like a turbocharger, for the extra burst of drive propelling us to our goals & success leading ultimately to the cultivation of a consciously-led habit of success. Making it a habit takes the mechanism back to the sub-conscious level for operational control and sets it effectively as the default operating mode put on autopilot.

However, dopamine merely provides the drive and the motivation but if we don't act on it is pointless. Thus, motivation has to be backed & supplemented by perseverance, persistence & domain competence to yield any meaningful results. However, with perseverance even the competence can be developed, honed & enhanced over time. If somebody's game, in terms of competence, confidence & morale, is already at the 100% level this extra boost would give that additional 20% as motivational edge which would prove to be an added & decisive advantage as a potential match winning inning over the competition on a given day.

Super Ordinate Goals in Business Context

The super-ordinate goal of reaching the space & landing the first man on moon, under U.S. President J.F. Kennedy, to ensure U.S.' lead in space domain over the Soviet Union; drove the scientists & engineers engaged in the U.S. space program under NASA to develop all the technologies & systems required from scratch in less than a decade from its announcement in May 1961 to Neil Armstrong's moon landing in July 1969. It was incredible given that the development of a modern fighter jet program in today's world takes almost 15 years from conception to entry into service.

The goal of developing a top of the line reconnaissance plane for the United States to provide effective tracking of Soviet Union's military activities at the peak of the Cold War in the early 1960s led Kelly Johnson and the Skunk Works team to outdo even themselves in the creation of the world's fastest (at Mach 3.2) & the highest flying aircraft (at 80,000 feet), the undisputed lord of the skies, the SR-71 Blackbird, while inventing almost all the technologies, tooling & production processes from scratch in just 20 months flat.

Super Ordinate Goals and Cricket

1. The Incredible Aussie Tribute to their 12th Man: One of the best examples of a super-ordinate goal in action on the cricket field was demonstrated effectively in the ODI World Cup of 2015, held in Australia & New Zealand, from February 14 to March 29, 2015. However, less than 3 months before the high profile event, Australian cricket had just witnessed one of its biggest blows. It came in form of the tragic & freakish demise of opener Phillip Hughes on the field in November 2014 off a short-pitched delivery which hit his helmet causing cerebral hemorrhage and death within days causing shock, grief and a wave of mourning across the nation. Australians were next scheduled to play the test series at home against India from November 24, 2014 to January 15, 2015, just prior to the world cup.

Australian captain, Michael Clark, and the team decided to pay tribute to Phil Hughes by naming him as the 13th man for the first two matches of the 3-match test-series against India. In the series, the Aussies simply outplayed India, playing under skipper MSD, and won the series 2-0. This was the series loss post which MSD announced his retirement from test cricket. The Aussies also wore black armbands in the series to commemorate Hughes.

The test series was followed by the Carlton Mid Triangular ODI Tri-Series; played between Australia, India and England; in which Australia and England met each other in the final with the Aussies comprehensively winning the tri-series. Team India lost 3 of the 4 games played by it and ended the forgettable series at the bottom of the points table. It was followed by the ODI World Cup, in which, the defending champions India clearly were coming off a rough patch while the Australians were on a mission, to play & win it for Hughes.

The Australians played the World Cup at a very different level altogether, wearing black armbands & giving their absolute best on the field. They simply outclassed almost every opponent in all departments of the game throughout the tournament, led by the pace of Mitchell Starc, who was almost unplayable and took 22 wickets to become the Player of the Tournament. The Aussies lost just 1 match through the group stages, to traditional arch-rivals, the Kiwis, who also had a super tournament with the exception of the final. Australia lost that match by a very narrow margin (NZ won by 1 wicket) in a rain affected match in the group stages of the tournament.

India, too, were turbocharged in the group stages and won all 6 of their matches comprehensively cruising to crush Bangladesh in the quarter final. In the semi-final, India, which had a fairly good tournament so far, faced the mighty Australians playing in the supercharged mode. The semi-final seemed somewhat of a repeat of the 2003's World Cup final saga with the Aussies putting 328 runs on the board batting first while India were scuttled for a mere 233 at Sydney with Dhawan making 45 off 41 balls, Rahane contributing with his 44 and Dhoni trying to steer the ship home with a run-a-ball 65 before getting run-out of a throw from Maxwell. However, when a team plays like that and for a special cause, there's very little an opposition team can do.

The Aussies routed traditional rivals, the Black Caps, in an almost one-sided final, wherein the Kiwis, batting first, were simply bowled out for 183 in just 45 overs. Australia comprehensively won the cup for the fifth time in 2015 with the skipper Michael Clarke describing Phil Hughes as the team's 16th man who played through the tournament while paying a tribute to Hughes in his post-win presentation speech. He said, "I'm sure everybody standing on this stage will say we played this World Cup with 16 players. This victory is dedicated to our little brother Phillip Hughes. Hughesy used to party as good as any of them so I guarantee we'll celebrate hard tonight."[40]

A similar phenomenon was seen at work during the 2016's T20 World Cup tournament, held in India, which was ultimately won by the dark horses of the game, the West Indies. However, more than the story of how they won the tournament, it is more important to know how they arrived for the tournament.

2. The Perfect Reply by the West Indies Cricket Team to their Board:

The West Indies' cricket players had an acrimonious dispute with the West Indies Cricket Board (WICB) over annual contracts[41] and pay just before the team set sail for India for the T20 World Cup. The WICB had been under a serious financial crunch and the players were provided with just a fraction of the sums due to them. The players were even threatened that the board would dispatch a second-rung team to play the tournament in their place. The team somehow managed to travel to India for the tournament and the players did not even have their team jerseys available with them when they arrived.

The board clearly did not value the players and the derided, insulted & beleaguered team was on its own without its patron. However, the team used it as the propulsive force to get to its goal of lifting the T20 world cup and thereby proving to the world that the board was wrong in its position as well as posture towards the players. The team played like champions through the tournament finishing at the top of the points table in their group, by winning 3 of their 4 matches, with the universe boss, Chris Gayle, slamming the fastest T20 century in the tournament of just 48 balls in their campaign opener against England.

The West Indies team subsequently derailed Sri Lanka, whirled past South Africa and stormed & stunned India in the semi-final match held at the Wankhede stadium with their explosive batting while chasing a daunting target of 192 in the semi-final. West Indies won the toss and elected to field, thus, becoming the only team to have chased this big a score in the knock out stages of a World T20 tournament. In the final, they outclassed England and successfully chased a target of 155 (while making 161 in turn) with two balls still spare with Marlon Samuels driving the team & the cup home with a fiery inning of 85 coming of just 66 balls. West Indies, thus, became the only team to have won the World Twenty20 twice.

The West Indies' captain, Darren Samy, recounted the tremendous odds faced by the team in its journey to the ultimate victory in the post match presentation. Another player from the West Indies' world cup winning team of 2016, Andre Fletcher, who spearheaded West Indies to victory with a batting average of 106[42] through the tournament, recently appeared in the Caribbean Cricket Podcast, and elaborated as to how the team channelized its dispute with the board to propel itself to becoming the world champions. He said, "Well if you know West Indies had a slogan - 'We versus them.' So we actually used that as a motivation and we were like, it is we the team versus the board. That's what we were saying."[42] The podcast further mentions the players saying that, "It felt like the team was more united than they had ever been." [43]

That's the power of the super-ordinate goal. In a clash of 'who wants it more' between the two teams on the field, it often boils down to the 'comparative strengths of the respective causes' they are battling it out for and most often victory favours the team with the relatively stronger & ideologically superior cause on a given day.

Team India's Unforgettable Farewell to their Legend

In the Indian cricket's context, the ODI World Cup of 2011 was a special occasion for two reasons. First, it was being held in India and second, it was the last world cup for the cricket legend, Sachin Tendulkar, who had been holding the reins of Indian cricket for over 2 decades. The Indian players wanted to give a befitting farewell to their super hero whom they had idolized as children seeing him on the television while growing up. The team wanted to be the first one ever to win it on home soil and give the World Cup itself as the souvenir and almost a parting gift to the little master. They worked for it through the tournament and took Indian cricket to its second ODI world cup win after 28 years.

The Player of the Series in that World Cup, Yuvraj Singh, recounted the rush of emotions overwhelming the Indian team, a decade back in 2011, in the following message posted by him in early April 2021 on his social media handle and reported by the media. He said, "The whole team wanted to win the World Cup so badly, especially for Sachin because we knew it was his last World Cup. We wanted to win the World Cup at home – which no other country had managed to do in the past. It was really special for us and I can't put it in words because those emotions can't be expressed."[44]

That more or less sums it up. It's the power of human emotions & relationships which is way stronger, as a propulsive force, than the glare of material goals or achievements. Some emotions can't be expressed in words; however, they can & should rather be channelized as the driving force to bring out our very best in the area where it matters most…

Phil Knight has brilliantly summed up the essence of the same in his memoir, Shoe Dog. He said. "It was never just business. It never will be. If it ever does become just business, that will mean that business is very bad. I keep thinking of one line in 'The Bucket List'. 'You measure yourself by the people who measure themselves by you."[79, 19]

Learning Principle: Play for the Bigger Cause

In a clash of 'who wants it more' between the two teams on the field, it often boils down to the 'comparative strengths of the respective causes' they are battling it out for and most often victory favours the team with the relatively stronger & ideologically superior cause on a given day.

CHAPTER VII

SUSTAINING LEADERSHIP - ADAPTING & EVOLVING ONE'S GAME INCREMENTALLY

Legendary boxing champion, Muhammad Ali, nicknamed 'The Greatest', started his professional career as a lightweight amateur boxer and won a gold medal at the 1960 summer Olympics held in Rome. This paved his onward journey, as a professional pugilist, to the heavyweight arena where he had a shot at the title of the World Heavyweight Championship in a clash against the defending champion, Sonny Liston, in 1964.

Ali (Cassius Clay back then), however, was somewhat unlike the usual image of a heavyweight boxer, with his agile body, constant movement around in the ring without settling down, which came to be known later, as the famous Ali Hussle, and also gave way to the famous adage, 'Float like a butterfly, sting like a bee; his hands can't hit what his eyes can't see', as said by Clay himself in 1964. This restless movement of his, combined with very sharp reflexes & lack of heavy punching power, led to his boxing style being regarded initially as a misfit for heavyweight boxing by the experts.

Additionally, his capability to withstand the enormous punching power of some of the reigning champions of the heavyweight league was also doubtful along with his ability to be able to fight inside. His unconventional boxing style, characterized by a low stance with hands staying low and his tendency to lean away from the incoming punches, had all been termed as fundamental technical flaws by the experts of the game.

The same was also reflected in the views of the sporting media covering the game at the time. Jimmy Cannon, the legendary columnist with the New York Journal - American newspaper at the time, had almost written a cryptic obituary for Ali's heavyweight boxing career with his view, "Clay doesn't fight like the valid heavyweight he is. He seldom sets and misses a lot. In a way, Clay is a freak. He is a bantamweight who weighs more than 200 pounds."[96]

Very logically, nobody gave Clay a chance in the battle of the heavyweights despite his impressive career record in the lightweight category of 19 wins & no loss, over the 3 year period spanning 1960 to 1963, with 15 of his wins coming from knock-outs. However, he had been knocked down twice by two hard hitting boxers, namely, Henry Cooper and Sonny Banks hitherto but he had managed to overwhelm both in the subsequent rounds to win the bouts eventually.

Clay himself said, 3 years later in 1966, prior to a key heavyweight boxing bout against Cleveland Williams, to media in an interview, "I don't have any [big] punch. I just hit a man so many times he wished I had a punch."[47] However, he went on to face & thrash some of the most ferocious, fiercest & hard-hitting boxers of all time, including, Sonny Liston, George Foreman, Floyd Patterson & Joe Frazier; to become the greatest boxing legend of all time, by the time he finished.

Another aspect of his game was that despite being an outlier; with an unconventional technique at the very outset of his heavyweight career, with one of the most unusual tactical approaches to heavyweight boxing, best captured by his phrase, 'float like a butterfly & sting like a bee'; he kept evolving it further. By the 1970s, almost a decade into the heavyweight league, Ali had developed a super punch which he used in his fight against Joe Frazier and also to knock down & knock-out Richard Dunn, the English, European and Commonwealth boxing champion, in 1976.

Ali learnt this super punch from the South Korean Taekwondo Grandmaster; Jhoon Rhee[48], who is also referred to as the Father of the American Taekwondo. Rhee called it the 'AccuPunch'[48] and, in fact, had learnt it directly from none other than the legendary 'Little Dragon', the greatest martial artist of all times, Bruce Lee, himself. The punch was extraordinarily fast and was almost impossible to block. It was in fact based on the premise that, 'the execution of the punch should be complete before the human brain can react with brain-to-wrist communication based on its standard reaction time'[48]. In a demonstration given by Rhee to Ali; Ali was himself unable to block the incoming punch, which came at him almost like a supersonic bullet.

In a media interview given on television, Ali had said, "I learned the Accupunch from Mr. Jhoon Rhee. It acts at the exact moment you decide to hit, and there is no lag time at all. It is instantaneous. It moves at tremendous speed with no warning and accelerates like a bullet in flight. You can hardly see it."[48] Apart from the AccuPunch, Bruce Lee also had his famous one-inch punch, which, when hit from a distance of just 1-inch from the opponent's body, would knock the man back by an incredible distance of almost 16 feet with the explosive impact force.

Tracing the approach of the creator of the AccuPunch, Bruce Lee, to fighting & life, one can easily see striking similarities between the two legends, Ali & Lee respectively.

First, they were both fighters and dabbled in poetry alongside. Second, they both were strong proponents of continuous evolution of one's game. Third, both had a life-changing event in the very same year, 1964. Ali fought and defeated Sonny Liston twice to become the World Heavyweight Champion of the world in 1964.

Bruce Lee, on the contrary, had been challenged for a duel by a renowned Chinese martial artist & teacher, Wong Jack Man, who was also in his early 20s at the time, just like Bruce Lee. The duel was to be held in the very same year, 1964, as the Chinese martial arts fraternity had been unhappy that Lee had been teaching martial arts to the non-Chinese in Seattle. The duel was held in private and was not recorded.

Bruce Lee did win the challenge comprehensively; however, he was not happy the way it had gone. According to the self-oriented perfectionist Lee, it took him much longer than it should have actually taken him to finish it and it troubled him that he could not live up to his true potential. As with all masters, his competition, too, was not with his opponents but rather with himself. This proved to be a major turning point in his life & career.

How Bruce Lee Reinvented His Game Fundamentally

What Bruce Lee did after that was to evolve his game to an altogether different realm where it was only him and the only real opponent he had for a duel was himself. He came to believe that there could be no specific martial art style which could harness the true potential of human body and mind working in unison and he had to, in turn, go way beyond the limitations imposed by the styles as none of them proved to be really effective in a consistent manner. He effectively pressed the reboot button and invented a unique philosophy of his own, drawing from the best practices & techniques of different styles as well as forms, and fusing them while also differentiating it effectively from the mixed martial arts style.

That philosophy of his has been known as 'Jeet Kune Do' or No Style for a Style or literally, "Using no way as way; having no limitation as limitation" as he famously said and meant 'being limitless', which ultimately became the core tenet of his martial arts' as well as life's philosophy. His philosophy was about expressing oneself fully & authentically while improvising in any given situation in life or martial arts.

Bruce Lee further elaborated about his 'Jeet Kune Do' philosophy in an article published in 1971 (just 2 years prior to his demise in 1973) in the Black Belt Magazine. He said, "I have not invented a "new style," composite, modified or otherwise that is set within distinct form as apart from "this" method or "that" method. On the contrary, I hope to free my followers from clinging to styles, patterns, or molds. Remember that Jeet Kune Do is merely a name used, a mirror in which to see "ourselves". . There is no mystery about my style. My movements are simple, direct and non-classical. The extraordinary part of it lies in its simplicity. Every movement in Jeet Kune Do is being so of itself. There is nothing artificial about it. I always believe that the easy way is the right way. Jeet Kune Do is simply the direct expression of one's feelings with the minimum of movements and energy. The closer to the true way of Kung Fu, the less wastage of expression there is."[97]

He actually relinquished the very concept of style by ascribing & treating it as a box and the biggest limiting factor of martial arts believing that every style imposes its own set of limitations & makes one more or less predictable & limited to a specific set of actions. These are like chinks in the armor which are then studied by the opponents as one's potential weaknesses which ultimately get exploited to the hilt and pave the way for defeat. This was Bruce Lee's process! His works and martial arts philosophy were compiled and published posthumously in 1975, in his book, Tao of Jeet Kune Do.

Bruce Lee summarized his philosophy of adapting, evolving & formlessness; for martial arts as well as life; using water as the metaphor, while quoting lines from the TV series, Longstreet, in which he had been playing a Jeet Kune Do master. The following excerpt from his last interview given to Pierre Berton, a Canadian journalist in 1971[50], captures his philosophy succinctly.

Lee had said:

"Be Water, My Friend.

Empty your mind.

Be formless, shapeless, like water.

You put water into a cup; it becomes the cup.

You put water into a bottle; it becomes the bottle.

You put it into a teapot; it becomes the teapot.

Now water can flow, or it can crash.

Be water, my friend."[49]

Bruce Lee's philosophy for martial arts & life has been captured holistically & effectively in the book, "Be Water, My Friend: The True Teachings of Bruce Lee", written by his daughter Shannon Lee.

Evolving & Reinventing One's Game and MSD

In the Cricketing realm, when a rookie Dhoni was looking to make it to the big league, his unconventional technique, too, was derided at by the experts of the game. While appearing for a selection for the Railway's[51] Ranji Trophy team, way back in 2002, he was rejected after keeping wickets for just 3 balls, with the selectors simply unimpressed by his keeping as well as batting, finding him technically not sound enough to represent the Railways cricket team.

Even when he had made his way to the national team, the wicket-keeping experts of the yore, found his unconventional technique behind stumps to be unsound, with the former Indian wicket-keeper, Syed Kirmani, leading the pack. He has commented on it in media interviews, as recently as 2018, saying "If you talk about collection of the throw. He has to go right behind the stumps, not what Dhoni does (sometimes he takes it from ahead of stumps). [Rishabh] Pant is following him. It is not a technique. You have to get behind in line with the stumps; your eye level should be in line with the bails to see where the ball is pitching so that you can judge it better"[52].

He further said, "MS Dhoni's wicket-keeping style should not be aped by youngsters."[52] However, Dhoni worked on his game & effectively proved it otherwise with his on-field results & impact, both behind as well as in front of the stumps, just as Ali did it inside the ring by facing & defeating some of the best pugilists, the sport has ever produced.

Dhoni started out as an explosive wicket-keeper batsman, who could turn the fat of the game with his bat in just a couple of overs, at any given juncture of the game. He was a maverick with the bat as well, with an unconventional technique, comprising a playbook of unorthodox shots, with the hallmark of the same being the helicopter shot, which he has used to great effect through his career.

However, he also evolved his game by transforming himself effectively from being the swashbuckler, mustang; who could also keep wickets, to the mature, wicket-keeper Captain Cool; seen today with his on-field presence, as the keeper and the captain, becoming the core of his game while batting has become relegated to a secondary role over the years.

That kind of evolution was necessary for him, from an evolutionary & longevity perspective, given that wicket-keeping is a tedious & laborious job requiring tremendous amount of focus, concentration & energy on every single ball. Thus, managing to think on one's feet, as the captain, on a sustained basis, along-with keeping wickets, is simply a herculean and a monumental task in itself for anyone especially with advancing age.

MSD had to further evolve his game and his role in the CSK team as visible in the IPL 2023. Nursing a painful knee, Dhoni has been batting at Number 7 in the CSK's batting order this time around as at this position he does not need to play more than just a couple of overs, wherein, he has to play to his typical strength, which is to hit big sixes and accelerate the scoring rate to take the team to a good score while batting first or help the team bridge the deficit between the runs required & balls remaining quickly while chasing. Further, this way, he doesn't need to undertake quick singles or doubles which might put pressure on his knee and he also does not need to face the spinners in the middle overs against whom he has been found to be struggling a bit over the past few IPL seasons. That way he gets to play his part behind the wickets in the fielding half of the game effectively, wherein, he brilliantly controls the game tactically.

Further, from a strategy perspective, the wicket-keeper's position is kind of a vantage point which provides the best possible positioning on the field to monitor, observe & control the game most effectively, if one is able to manage & sustain the additional workload that comes along with it. That is why we haven't really seen many wicket-keeper captains in the game historically. However, the IPL has been a clear exception to the same with the IPL 2021 now having four out of the eight participating teams being captained by wicket-keepers. These include K.L. Rahul for Punjab Kings, Sanju Samson for Rajasthan Royals, MSD for CSK and Rishabh Pant for Delhi Capitals.

The emergence of wicket-keeping captains in cricket, has been explored in a recent article[53], appearing in 'The Hindu', which sought views from the English wicket-keeper batsman, Jos Buttler, about the growing trend. Buttler concurs with the view, that a wicket-keeper indeed gets the best, 360 degree view of the game with his tremendous positional advantage and this provides a definite edge to the keeping captains. Buttler said, "I think a wicketkeeper has a brilliant view of the game. That can add to your decision-making as you can see first-hand how the wicket is behaving and the way bowlers are bowling."[53]

Buttler further ascribed the growing trend of wicket-keeping captains, in the IPLs, to MSD saying that, "I am sure MSD (Dhoni) has something to do with the sixth sense and breeding of wicketkeepers who can captain. He obviously has been a fantastic captain and there are lots of players who want to follow his footsteps."[53]

Evolving & Reinventing One's Game and Cricket

Talking about resilience & evolution of one's game, one can't help but think about the English seam bowler, Stuart Broad, who had a disastrous take-off to his bowling career as he was clobbered & almost butchered by Yuvraj Singh, who hit six sixes of a single over from Broad in the Twenty20 World Cup of 2007. Broad was literally at his wits' end, during & after that horrendous ordeal.

Yuvraj recounted that match & the inning in a BBC podcast last year and recalled how Broad's father, Chris Broad, told him that he might have put an end to his son's career. Yuvraj said, "His dad, Chris Broad, is a match referee and he came up to me the next day and said 'you almost finished my son's career and now you need to sign a shirt for him. So I gave my India jersey and wrote a message for Stuart saying, 'I have been hit for five sixes so I know how it feels. For the future of England cricket, all the best.'[54].

Stuart, however, made a remarkable comeback from that brutal assault and pulverizing blow, worked on his game tremendously and transformed eventually into becoming only the third English bowler, and seventh bower in cricket's history, to have taken 500 wickets in test cricket, a feat which he achieved in July 2020. Even Yuvraj himself said to BBC, "Stuart is one of the best bowlers in the world now. I don't think any bowler from India could get hit for six sixes in an over and then have such a fantastic career"[54].

Even Lasith Malinga, the Sri Lankan pace bowler, well-known for his precise, laser-guided & almost rocket propelled Yorkers, adapted his bowling in the later years of his career when he had lost his speed. He limited himself to the shorter, T20 format of the game, wherein he only had to bowl 4 overs and he focused more on accuracy & variations, rather than speed, which had been his original weapon of choice as the weapon master.

Unfortunately, there are some who get consumed by the 'unchecked ego' on their way to the top and develop the disease called 'me' which effectively stalls their growth journey & impairs the ability to be an effective team player. The unchecked ego, thus, puts them effectively on the path of stagnation & ultimately extinction as they stop learning & growing as disciplined professionals. In the aviation world, there have been numerous pilots who developed big egos and considered themselves way superior & above the well laid-out procedures, checklists & safety procedures. They hated flying with new hires, considering them as lesser flying beings, with corollaries relevant & applicable for other domains as well as areas.

In this context, a quote from English football coach and former Arsenal player & captain, Tony Adams, comes like the silver bullet. He said, "Play for the name on the front of the shirt, and they'll remember the name on the back."[80] He was Arsenal's captain for 14 long years and captain of the England's national football team from 1992-1996. It was simply his humility and love for Arsenal which turned him into an icon of the game, which could be gauged from his quote of 2013. He had said, "It's my football club, Arsenal Football Club. When I'm needed, when I'm wanted, I'll make the tea there!"[80]

That invariably reminds one of MSD, who once actually drove the team bus himself; as recalled & narrated by VVS Laxman in the Star Sports' Cricket Connected chat show. In 2008, during India's test series against Australia, Dhoni actually drove the team bus from the stadium to the team hotel in Nagpur.

Laxman said, "He was the captain of the Indian team because Anil

[Kumble] announced his retirement two matches before in Delhi (in 2008). And MS Dhoni asked the team bus driver to just go and sit behind, and he drove the team bus from the ground to the hotel in Nagpur, and we were all awestruck. The captain of the Indian team, driving the team bus!"[81]

This is the Maverick side of his persona and the game which has given him that decisive edge over others in close, tight or tricky situations on the field. Laxman further said about Dhoni's humility, "That's how he used to enjoy his life. For him, being a cricketer was doing everything on the cricket field, but outside the field, everything was normal."[81]

There have been other Indian players as well, who effectively developed antibodies and subsequent immunity against this ego disease, and have kept cruising steadily on their evolutionary path.

In Indian cricket, Virat Kohli's transformation of his batting, post India's 2011's World Cup victory & over the subsequent years; into the relentless run machine that he has been since then; marked by the ingestion of discipline, commitment, fitness & improvisation; has propelled him to effectively scale & summit the peak of the game.

This is what Virat Kohli had to say about his personal transition & the journey chasing excellence in a media interview given in May 2019, "Soon after 2012. That's the year when the transition began. It began more with the idea of inculcating a stricter sense of discipline and need for fitness. When I started my own transition in fitness the simple realization was that if I don't keep up with the demands of the game, I'm going to be an average cricketer. People will remember me as someone who did well for three or four years and then, kind of, was one among the many. I knew that I had to change everything about my life, about myself, to be able to be at the top of my game, to be in sync where the world (of sport) is heading."[86]

Talking about evolution & improvisation, both Virat Kohli and Sachin Tendulkar, kept evolving & improvising their game, as batsmen, through the incorporation of small, tactical changes & improvements throughout, including the addition of some new shots to their already vast arsenal of shots, which effectively limited the ability of the bowlers to study their respective games as a static construct & exploit weaknesses.

They remained dynamic, kept learning & evolving their game throughout and that's why they have been so effective & successful with Virat still going strong.

As Bruce Lee has said, in sports as well as in life, the opponents will study your game looking to expose your weaknesses & exploit them and it happens eventually to everyone.

However, the masters keep working hard on themselves as well as their game and eventually turn their weaknesses into strengths with their sheer perseverance, discipline & determination and that is what makes them extraordinary & ultimately sets them apart from the ordinary. Thus, the only real competition one has is with oneself, with focus on realizing true potential, by becoming a better version of one's own self by growing incrementally with time.

Harbhajan Singh's creation of Doosra and R. Ashwin's conception of the Carrom ball; effectively expanded their variations, took their game to a different level and eventually proved critical in their career successes. Similarly, Suresh Raina and Gautam Gambhir's perceived weaknesses against short bowling became well known and were exploited effectively by the bowlers against them. Even MSD has been curtailed to some extent by the bowlers, for some years now, who have been bowling precise Yorkers to him outside the off-stump or have been weaving spin webs of-late to trap him and, so far, he has seemed rickety & vulnerable against these tactics.

However, this striving for excellence & perfection, should be self-driven & intrinsically-motivated rather than being socially prescribed, as the research into perfection has identified so far, to have a really healthy relationship with overall motivation. The extrinsically-driven approaches, on the contrary, mostly lead to anxiety & confidence issues. Also, the pursuit of perfection & excellence is a double-edged sword, which could result in significant self-harm, if left unchecked or taken to the extreme, where it becomes an obsession & the driving force operating in the autonomous mode, causing delays & becoming an impediment to progress. Balance, thus, is the key here and incremental, the keyword.

The essence, in a nutshell, is that Evolution is life and Stagnation, simply the beginning of the end. A student of the game & life never stops learning.

To the legend, Bruce Lee, who has put it beautifully:-

"Be Water, My Friend..."[49]

Learning Principle

In sports as well as in life, the opponents will study your game looking to expose your weaknesses & exploit them and it happens eventually to everyone. However, the masters keep working on themselves and eventually turn their weaknesses into strengths with their perseverance, discipline & determination and that is what makes them extraordinary & ultimately sets them apart from the ordinary.

CHAPTER - VIII

SITUATIONAL LEADERSHIP – THE BALANCING ACT BETWEEN TASK FOCUS & THE TEAM INTERESTS

The Situational Leadership Model

The classic Situational Leadership model®; developed by Dr. Paul Hersey & Ken Blanchard, postulates that there is no absolutely perfect leadership style and the leader has to adapt his style, based on the situation & the task at hand; while incorporating performance readiness & willingness level of his team members into the overall equation; with task and people as the two core tenets of the theory.

The model says that the leader's style should range from directing, for the teammates who lack the skill but are willing to learn, to delegation for the seasoned campaigners, who are skilled at the job, confident, motivated & willing to take responsibility. For the individuals, who are somewhere in between these two opposite ends of the spectrum, i.e., have limited willingness or ability, the leaders should use the participatory style for the former while for the latter, the ones who are confident but have limited ability, the leader should use the selling leadership style.

MSD & Situational Leadership

MSD's leadership covered all these styles, throughout his captaincy career, and varied, based on the situations faced, with him helping the spin bowlers, especially, Kuldeep, Chahal & Jadeja from behind the stumps, being the hallmark of directing. However, his intent was & has always been to help the bowlers with his experience to adapt & optimize their bowling as per the pitch, conditions and the juncture of the match for maximum impact. Real directing, selling or participatory styles would come into play when they would be going off-course by not bowling in the right areas, not bowling as per the field, unwilling to pitch it up or not thinking straight.

He summed up his theory & approach to managing the bowlers with the following statement given in a media interview to ESPN CricInfo, way back in 2008. He had said, "I give first preference to the bowler. I ask them for their fields and they say, "Okay, this is the field I want." And if it's a first-change bowler, for example, then I will tell him, "Look, this is what is happening." Maybe Irfan or Praveen Kumar ... I will tell Irfan, "Very little chances of you bringing the ball in, maybe the ball will slide away. So you can think of this field." Whatever I can suggest. The initial balls he will bowl according to his field - according to what he thinks will happen. Then if he's not successful with his field, that's the time I step in and say, "Okay, this is it, now you have to bowl according to my field. Because your plan is not working. So this is the plan that's been given to you and you should be bowling to it." He may be happy about it or not"[32].

Dhnoi's style thus ranged from delegating to directing with the switching decision contingent on & triggered by the on-field scenario & situational demands.

MSD's approach remained the same over the following years, as evinced by his statement given in another interview, given to bcci.tv, six years later in 2014. He said, "I don't like to give a plan that the bowler is not comfortable implementing. So I let the bowlers start off with their own plan and own fields and encourage them to think for themselves."[84]

He explained his tactical approach to communicating with the players on the field about specific aspects of the game in the same interview he had given in March 2008 to ESPN CricInfo after winning the T20 World Cup. He said, when asked about communicating his idea of the floating batting order to players, "I keep it very simple: "This is the thing I want and that's the way it'll go." So instead of going there and explaining too many things and confusing yourself and confusing him, it's important to make it very simple. At the international level you have guys who've played a lot - either at the domestic or at the international level - so I don't really believe in telling them too many things or making everything clear - they are clever enough to know what is happening and what are the demands of the game. That's one of my theories. I think it's working"[32]. That's how things have been under him even now as he has kept the communication & things really simple.

The style mentioned here, again, has been a hybrid of directing & delegating, rather than outright handholding or spoon-feeding; based on the premise that the players are seasoned & mature. It has been very similar to the way he took things in his own hands in the final of the 2011's World Cup, when he said to the team coach Gary Kirsten to tell Yuvraj that he (Dhoni) would be going out to bat up the order, before Yuvi, as the Sri Lankan spinners had been on the prowl.

However, bringing on rookies, raring to go to the fore at critical junctures of the game, is the real litmus test for any leader. MSD even perfected that art & mastered it with his instinctive approach to the game, honed by him, by practicing & applying it often in real-life, on-field scenarios. However, his unusual calls on the field and strokes with the bat were based on accurate, snap calculations & the fingertip feel anchored in deep experience and powered by one of the finest cricketing brains in the game with almost infinite processing speed & capacity.

His decision to bowl Joginder Sharma twice, back to back, in the semi final & final of the World Twenty20, has been the hallmark of this abstract theory of his. The decisions, however, were not just contrived tactical surprises but in fact were based on Sharma's ability to bowl full and at a pace which was hard for the batsman to hit, somewhat like the former New Zealand bowler, Gavin Larsen, who was well known for his economical bowling (which always delivered) and for being hard to hit, which duly earned him the nickname, 'The Postman', given by his teammates.

The unique characteristics of Joginder Sharma's bowling, coupled with the high pressure of the prevailing situation at death, along-with the precision of Dhoni's tactical guidance system collectively would have increased the probabilities of the batsman mis-timing & mis-hitting the balls which would have gone in India's favour.

That's simply what happened in that last over & last ball of the final. It has been Dhoni's uncanny ability to read the game superbly and the preciseness of matching & deploying resources aligned with the situation in real-time; which has led to such tactical brilliance in action, on the field on multiple occasions.

Ashish Nehra shed further light on this exceptional ability of MSD.

Nehra said, "He had a crystal clear idea about his go-to bowlers in slog overs, the shaky ones who could be clobbered at the death. That's called mind reading and you can't beat MS Dhoni on that. If he knew that a player had limited abilities, he would use him accordingly without being frustrated or abusing him and that's leadership."[82]

Indian cricket's one of the most controversial cricket coaches, Greg Chappell, who was at play from 2005-2007, when the maverick Dhoni was at the peak of his batting prowess, had said about Dhoni, "he had the gambler's streak that set the fine captains apart from the ordinary ones. "He's not reckless. Some of the shots he plays may seem outrageous and risky, but I can assure you he's usually weighed up the options. He knows what he's doing."[64]

MSD, as a leader, thus, has been a patron of Delegating first in the tactical aspects of the game and switching to Directing, if the former seems to be going wayward. However, in the strategic aspects of the game, he has simply been 'Directing' the show.

Balancing Task & People Focus – Leadership Grid

The leader has to balance the two core aspects (task & people) and walk the thin tightrope right in the middle, as also outlined by management theorists & authors, Blake & Mouton, in their Managerial Grid or Leadership Grid model, where they also recommend the balancing act, with their Middle-of-the-Road ideology, of balancing focus on task with concern for people.

However, as per the Managerial Grid, the most effective leadership style is 'Team Management', in which, the leader is passionate about and committed to achieving organizational goals & missions. He inspires, motivates & empowers his team members to work towards achieving the goal while simultaneously also caring & looking after them.

Leaders, however, sometimes tend to err in perfecting this delicate balancing act in their relentless pursuit of operational excellence. In the 2012's ODI tri-series held in Australia; the decision to adopt rotation policy for the Top-3 slots in team India's batting order, with 3 senior Indian players; namely, Virender Sehwag, Sachin Tendulkar & Gautam Gambhir; getting termed as relatively slow fielders on huge Australian outfields, as per media reports, created major internal turbulence & fissures within the team, with the entire episode subsequently erupting into a major controversy for Indian cricket.

One of the senior players, Virender Sehwag, told CricBuzz in a recent interview, given in 2020, that sometimes even MSD failed to communicate effectively, he said, "When MS Dhoni said in Australia that top three are slow fielders, we were never asked or consulted. We got to know from the media. He said at the press conference but not at the team meeting that we are slow fielders."[76]

Gen. Mattis, however, had a clear take on this delicate, balancing act and he was known for his advice of caution to leaders to not allow & let their passion for excellence destroy their compassion for their subordinates[77]. He further says, "Everyone needs a coach, but nobody needs a tyrant."[35]

The Balancing Act and Shackleton's Expeditions

In this context, the leadership of the legendary English explorer, Sir Ernest Shackleton, as witnessed over the course of his four adventurous expeditions to the South Pole, over a century ago, clearly stands out and has almost become a case study in resilient leadership. He typically would always put the safety & welfare of his men above everything else and that became evident in the outcomes of his hazardous missions in terms of returning head counts.

In his first, 4-men mission, christened Nimrod, in 1907-09, they were within sniffing distance of their destination, the South Pole, and just 97 miles away when Shackleton took the momentous decision, while braving atrocious weather conditions & battling exhaustion, to abandon the mission & the beckoning glory and instead decided to head back, as they lacked sufficient food supplies to get back home safely.

In the 'Endurance' mission, which set sail 5-years later in 2014, he again successfully led his 28-men crew; who were mostly novices, outlaws & ordinary seafarers accompanied by scientists; back home to safety after their ship was decimated by ice, with his 'Fortitudine Vincimus' philosophy, literally meaning 'by fortitude we become victorious', while withstanding & literally enduring enormous adversities in the freezing polar hell and keeping the morale & spirits high throughout the over 2-years long ordeal. That's why it has been duly termed as the world's greatest real story of survival & leadership and explains as to why his crew called him, 'The Boss'.

Shackleton, thus, has deservingly become the subject of microscopic examination of modern leadership researchers, management hawks & business schools globally looking to crack the code of resilient leadership and seeking some crucial & invaluable lessons in leadership for hard times.

The acclaimed British scientist, Sir Raymond Priestley, who served with Captain Robert Falcon Scott & Ernest Shackleton on Antarctic expeditions, has said about Shackleton. He said, "For scientific leadership, give me

Scott. For swift and efficient travel, Amundsen. But when you are in a hopeless situation, when there seems no way out, get on your knees and pray for Shackleton." Author Michael Smith has chronicled the life, leadership & expeditions of Shackleton in his excellent book, "Shackleton: By Endurance We Conquer".

Coming back to MSD; post the adventurous, icy detour, MSD has always valued & embraced confidence, motivation & unconventionality, despite skill limitations and has persisted, while side-stepping embattled rank & credentials battling morale issues, to drive extraordinary results.

He firmly believes that confident & motivated newcomers can be far greater assets and game changers at critical junctures, despite their skill limitations, than well-established players battling confidence and moral issues.

Harnessing 'Black Sheep' Potential at Pixar

A similar approach was adopted by Pixar's director, Brad Bird, when confronted with daunting animation challenges, while taking on the animated movie, The Incredibles, as unveiled in an interview given by hime to McKinsey & Company in April 2008. Brad harnessed the latent creative potential of the restless animators inside Pixar, who were teeming with unconventional ideas & raring to go, terming them as the Black Sheep, and pushing them hard to think out-of-the box and go beyond their comfort zones.

Steve Jobs, who also owned Pixar, had hired Brad Bird way back in 2000 to disrupt things at Pixar. He had told Bird while hiring him, "The only thing we're afraid of is complacency—feeling like we have it all figured out. We want you to come shake things up."[63]

When Brad Bird finally set out to take on 'The Incredibles' challenge; he had said, "Give us the black sheep. I want artists who are frustrated. I want the ones who have another way of doing things that nobody's listening to. Give us all the guys who are probably headed out the door." A lot of them were malcontents because they saw different ways of doing things, but there was little opportunity to try them, since the established way was working very, very well."[63].

He further added, "We gave the black sheep a chance to prove their theories, and we changed the way a number of things are done here. For less money per minute than was spent on the previous film, *Finding Nemo*, we did a movie that had three times the number of sets and had everything that was hard to do. All this because the heads of Pixar gave us leave to try crazy ideas."[63]

Brad Bird's advice on creating a culture of disruption & innovation, as a Leader, 'Herd your Black Sheep'[63].

MSD's take, too, has been quite similar, 'Bet on the Mustangs & the Dark Horses, while backing and nudging them tactically, to win the high-stakes Derbies'.

Learning Principle – Focus on the Task while Caring for People

A leader has to balance the two core aspects (task & people) and walk the thin tightrope right in the middle with the most effective leadership style being 'Team Management', in which, the leader is passionate about and committed to achieving organizational goals & missions. He inspires, motivates & empowers his team members to work towards achieving the goal while simultaneously also caring & looking after them. However, the

Leaders should not allow & let their passion for excellence destroy their compassion for their subordinates.

CHAPTER - IX

COURSES FOR HORSES – THE LONG-TERM PLAY - TURNING ORDINARY STALLIONS INTO GAME-CHANGERS

'Courses for Horses', in terms of phraseology, sounds much like the clichéd, 'Horses for Courses', which everybody has been doing typically & traditionally for ages. However, the difference between the two emanates from the perspective or the way of approaching things. While the latter focuses on things from a task & resource deployment perspective (with telling & directing as traditional cornerstones), the former takes a people/relationship oriented perspective (guided by communication & engagement); under the Situational Leadership model by taking a long term view of things and basing decisions on the respective strengths & weaknesses of each horse in the stable from an absolute, developmental & long-term perspective. The phrase, 'Courses of Horses', thus, is more like the inducement of a second-order change into the system.

Talking about horses, linguistically & figuratively, they come in a range of sizes & types. In the lexicon, there are Workhorses, War Horses, Dark Horses, Mustangs, Racehorses, Stallions and the Prancing Horses, apart from, of course, the Colts. There are also the mythical & mystical ones, in the form of Pegasus & Unicorns. Each one of them is distinctly unique in psyche, character, self-identity and real-world applications. A mustang can't do consistently what a workhorse can and similarly a war horse can't be deployed on a racetrack & expected to win the way a racehorse would and vice-versa.

This (role specialization), seemingly, is almost contradictory to the concept of being formless & limitless. However, the point is that the journey for everyone starts from the box and greatness lies in breaking out of the mould by transcending the boundaries & limitations imposed by the form and carving a true niche for oneself eventually.

The Extraordinary Transformation of an American Racehorse

In the America of the early 1930s, reeling under the economic gloom of the Great Depression, there was a tiny colt in Kentucky, named, Seabiscuit, with the bizarre & incongruous name for a racehorse coming from his father, Hard Tack, which is a type of biscuit used often by sailors on long sea voyages. Seabiscuit's trainer saw potential in the colt but felt that the horse was indolent.

Seabiscuit had a disastrous start to his racing career by losing the first 17 races miserably and finishing almost at the very end in most of them. He won just 10 of his first 40 races and had clearly been performing way below his potential. He was, thus, sold by his original owners in 1936 owing to sub-par performance. The new owners assigned Seabiscuit to a new trainer, Tom Smith, who was well known for his unconventional training methods as the 'mustang breaker'.

Tom had trained horses, as a young man, for the United States Cavalry and was also known by the nickname, 'Silent Tom', for his quiet nature. Tom worked with Seabiscuit using his unorthodox techniques to bring him out of his laziness and, in turn, paired him with the seasoned Canadian jockey, Red Pollard, who had failed as a professional boxer earlier and was also blind in one eye.

Under Howard and Pollard, Seabiscuit had a virtual transformation and in 1937, within a year, he had won 11 of his 15 races. Seabiscuit, temperamentally, was an easy starter who would stick with the pack & hold but would pull up later in the race with great acceleration. Racing legend has it that if Seabiscuit looked at a competing horse in the eye while running on the track nothing could defeat him after that. The Seabiscuit, thus, had a competitive streak to his racing. However, the easy starter part was a great disadvantage in head-to-head races, held traditionally between just two horses and termed as match racing, which usually favor the horse managing to take a head start over the opponent.

In November 1938, Seabiscuit was scheduled to take on his arch-rival, 'War-Admiral', in a head-to-head race to be held at the Pimlico Race Course in Baltimore, Maryland. Seabiscuit clearly had been an underdog with the 'War Admiral', an old foe, well known for his lightning take-off speed, right at the outset and, thus, was considered almost invincible by the media after having won the 'Triple Crown' and named as the 'American Horse of the Year' for the year 1937.

Seabiscuit's trainer, Tom Smith, trained his racehorse for this head-to-head, match-race race format by using Psychology's famous learning theory and technique, referred to as classical conditioning, which is named after Ivan Pavlov, a Russian physiologist. Smith used a starting bell and a whip and conditioned Seabiscuit for an almost full afterburner powered take-off, right from the gate, while transforming his game fundamentally in the process.

The head-to-head clash, known as match racing, between Seabiscuit and the War Admiral, was a grand event and was dubbed as the 'Match of the Century' and 'Pimlico Special'; which drew huge crowds with the area almost bursting at the seams.

The spectators' & media's craze and the public frenzy for the event were simply unprecedented & almost hysteric. Almost the entire nation had come to a standstill for the face-off between the two legendary racehorses. Special trains were run to bring almost 40,000 fans & spectators from all across the country while the radio broadcast was tuned in to by about 40 million people across the globe.

Even the U.S. President, Franklin D Roosevelt (FDR), had been gripped by the match-race fever and the match of the century. A media article reported, "During a cabinet meeting, (FDR) had stopped all business of presiding over the nation to listen to the radio broadcast of a race between two horses 40 miles up the road in Baltimore. FDR, like an estimated 40 million people listening around the world, was captivated by the match race at Pimlico Race Course between Seabiscuit and War Admiral – one of the most anticipated sporting events of the 20th century."[100]

Laura Hillenbrand, author of the bestselling book on Seabiscuit published in 1999, said about the race in a media interview published in The Guardian, "Horse racing was in its heyday, and Seabiscuit was an enormous cult hero."[100] She further added, "They didn't know what to do with all the people. They funneled 10,000 people into the infield. People were hanging from the rafters in the grandstand. Thousands more were outside the track, hanging from trees, standing on rooftops. All of America was holding its breath for this race."[100]

Further, Seabiscuit hated muddy tracks and preferred to race on hard tracks instead. It had been raining heavily & incessantly in Baltimore during the days leading up to the race day and the track had been muddy. However, the jockey, George Woolf (Pollard's friend), who had been roped in by Tom Smith to replace an injured Pollard for the race, checked the track on the night before the race and found one particular track along the rail which was hardened and he chose this one for Seabiscuit's crusade.

Seabiscuit had a great start to the race and he took the lead right away following the starting bell and sustained it for a while. Sea Admiral, however, was a resilient foe and started catching up & reducing the gap mid-way before going on to take a slight lead. The jockey, knowing well about Seabiscuit, allowed him to have a look at War Admiral, in the eye, before prodding him to push further. Seabiscuit responded and went full throttle, just 200 yards from the finish line, almost like a tracer bullet, while taking the lead and sustaining it to the end for a grand & thoroughly well-deserved win. It was despite the fact that War Admiral had clocked his best time ever for the distance.

1938, thus, became the best year ever for Seabiscuit, in which, he was named 'American Horse of the Year', owing to his astounding run of successes through that year. By the time he finished his racing career in April 1940, Seabiscuit had become the top money-winning racehorse up to the 1940s. He was voted into the National Museum of Racing & Hall of Fame in 1958 and in 1999, he ranked 25th in the Blood-Horse magazine's list of the Top 100 U.S. racehorses of the 20th century. Interestingly, Seabiscuit also deservingly carried his unconventional trainer, Tom Smith, into the Blood Horse magazine's 'Hall of Fame' in the year 2000 with

Smith's induction (in 2001) based on voting by the members of the prestigious magazine's historic review committee.

Seabiscuit has almost been immortalized as the horse racing's legendary hero with a cult status & following, and has been the subject of multiple documentaries, non-fiction books and Hollywood films. The bestselling book, Seabiscuit: An American Legend, authored by Laura Hillenbrand, published in 1999 has captured the story vividly & exceptionally well, and was followed by the 2003's Hollywood movie, Seabiscuit; based on the same book, that was nominated for the Academy Award for Best Picture.

In the Indian context, a commensurate and, in fact, an even greater equine legend, comes not from the racetrack but rather from the heat of the battlefield, and it's about Chetak, the fiery, extremely loyal & royal steed of the legendary ruler of Mewar, Maharana Pratap. Chetak, despite getting injured in the Battle of Haldighati, carried his beloved master to safety with an incredible, giant leap across the raging stream before succumbing to his wounds ultimately. The stories of his extraordinary courage, loyalty & exemplary bravery have been an integral part of the regional folklore & have been recounted in the court poems of Mewar since the 17th century. Haldi Ghati even hosts a Chetak memorial (Samadhi), where Chetak was buried, built to commemorate the legendary warhorse and the structure is standing in fairly good condition even to this day. The place was visited frequently by Maharana Pratap during his subsequent years of forest dwelling with the Bhils.

The Transformation of a Mustang in Indian Cricket and MSD the Master Tactician

In Indian cricket, there has been a particular cricketer, whose story somehow mirrored and has been quite similar to Seabiscuit. When he first came into the national side in 2007 everyone knew that he had loads of talent, potential & promise. However, he was raw, brash, an easy starter & impulsive and would very often gift his wicket away after settling down with scores in mid-20s or early 30s by playing a rash shot which would not really be required in the situation. In fact, talent became a nickname cum pejorative for him on media & social media. Then, the magical touch of MSD came who had believed in his potential throughout and kept backing him along with selectors.

MSD asked him to open the innings in early 2013 in the home series against England and he looked solid in that inning, in which he made 80 runs. The move was taken a step further by MSD when he asked him to bat in the ICC's Champions Trophy of 2013, held in England.

The move could have backfired as opening the innings in swinging English conditions is usually tricky and requires quick adaptation in one's batting technique to cover it effectively. However, he did not disappoint and made two half-centuries in the tournament by scoring 65 against South Africa and 52 against the West Indies. He never looked back since then, has scored 29 hundreds in his ODI career so far and has been the only IPL captain so far to have won the title 5 times. He is none other than the Hitman, Rohit Sharma!

Look at the stark contrast in his batting as an opener vs. as a middle order batsman. As an opener, he has scored 7000+runs in 143 ODI matches with a staggering batting average of 57.44, whereas, his batting average, while batting in the middle order (from no. 4-7), has been a tardy 34.2 in 75 matches played from 2007-2012. However, the important point is that 27 of his 29 ODI career centuries and 3 double-hundreds in ODIs; have all come while opening the innings, with two of his three double hundreds coming within the first 2 years of becoming an opening batsman.

Rohit himself believes that it was a masterstroke which changed the course of his career & life forever. He shared the view in a media interview in early 2017. He said, "I believe the decision to open in ODIs changed my career and it was a decision taken by MS Dhoni. I became a better batsman after that. In fact, it helped me understand my game better, react better according to situations."[55] Rohit further added as to how the decision was communicated to him by MSD in his typical manner, as recounted by the Hitman, "He (Dhoni) just came up to me and said 'I want you to open the innings as I am confident that you will do well. Since you can play both cut and pull shot well, you have the qualities to succeed as an opener'."[55] Rohit further explained, "He told me that I shouldn't be scared of failures or get upset by criticism. He was looking at the bigger picture as the Champions Trophy was scheduled in England that year."[55]

Even Yuvraj Singh thanks Dhoni for letting the mustang go wild on the track with his bat. He said in a media interview, "Thanks mate! (Referring to Dhoni), Thanks for giving me the opportunity to slog as always."[56]

The Story of Transformations in Indian Cricket

Another Déjà vu moment for Indian cricket as a similar tactical move, made 26 years ago in 1994, had brought Sachin Tendulkar up the batting order, had altered the course of cricket in India. However, back then, it was Sachin himself, who almost pleaded to captain, Mohd. Azharuddin, for the change.

Recounting the pivotal moment of his career; Sachin said in a media interview, "In 1994, when I started opening the batting for India, the strategy used by all teams was to save wickets. What I tried to do was slightly out of the box. I thought I could go up front and take the opposition bowlers on. But I had to beg and plead to give me a chance. If I fail, I won't come after you again. In that first match (against New Zealand at Auckland), I scored 82 off 49 balls, so I didn't have to ask again if I would get another chance."[57] Prior to that, Sachin had played 69 ODI matches and he had been averaging just over 30 without having scored even a single of his 49 career centuries. Post that, his batting average rocketed up to almost 50.

A similar move, that turned out to be another game changer, had to be made by Dada & coach John Wright back in 2001, when he almost forced Sehwag, who preferred batting in the middle order, to open the innings as Sachin was ruled out of a match due to injury. When Sachin came back, he volunteered to bat at No. 4 to make way for Sehwag at the top.

Former Indian wicket-keeper batsman, Ajay Ratra, shared the same in a conversation with HT. He said, "Sachin was doing so well as an opener at that time but Sehwag had to open. So Sachin offered to bat at No.4. Sehwag then opened with Dada (Sourav Ganguly) for that left and right combination. If Sachin hadn't agreed then Viru probably would have had to bat lower. He wouldn't have got the chance to open in ODIs and the story could have been a lot different." [60] The Sehwag chapter, thus, had serendipitous origins and turned out to be a by-product of adversity rolled out purely by collective effort.

Transformation of Ravindra Jadeja under MSD

Even Ravindra Jadeja had a complete transformation under MSD from an underrated, dark horse to a top all-rounder & a virtual game changer with immense capability to virtually turn the game on its head with the ball, bat or with his fielding.

Jadeja also said in a recent interview that, 'It has been MSD who carves him to be the best version of him'[58]. He also mentioned about his initial hiccups with shot selection early on in his career and how Dhoni helped him overcome it by advising him, "I remember he said that I was trying to hit shots against balls I shouldn't be attempting."[58]

He further added, "Shot selection was something I also felt I was doing wrong. My judgment at the start wasn't right. I would be in double mind. 'Should I go for the shot or no?' These days, I like to take my time and I am clearer in my mind. I know I can always cover up the runs later. That change in thinking has helped."[58]

This is what MSD had to say about Jadeja, way back in Feb 2014 and look at the results he has been delivering with the bat over the recent years. Dhoni said, "It is vital for him to improve as a batsman. He has tremendous potential and the more games he plays, the better he'll get. It isn't about putting too much pressure on him, but it is important that he keeps working on his batting. Once he starts contributing with the bat consistently, we may have a different scenario. We may even look to play with five bowlers outside the subcontinent."[59] That is precisely how it has scripted out for Indian cricket over the recent years with Jadeja becoming an indispensable part of Team India's force structure.

MSD also helped CSK pace bowler, Deepak Chahar, transform into a power play bowling specialist as he saw tremendous potential in him for that and Chahar has turned out to be a great strike bowling asset for CSK over the years. This is exactly what Sourav Ganguly did for Indian cricket at the turn of the century having produced multiple game changers & champions, with some of the stalwarts being Yuvraj Singh, Virender Sehwag, Harbhajan Singh, Zaheer Khan, Ashish Nehra & Dhoni himself. However, MSD, as the worthy successor, took the process a notch further up by at least a single order of magnitude.

The point is, as the leader, it is not just about helping other players improve their game incrementally but rather about assessing, enabling & facilitating a complete transformation, with an evolution & effective transition to a unique niche meant for them, geared towards realizing their true potential in the process. Thus, transforming & turning ordinary stallions into truly game changers for the long-term.

That's what simply sets MSD a class apart from everyone else…and the difference will be felt forever by the game…

Learning Principle

As the leader, it is not just about helping other players improve their game incrementally but rather about assessing, enabling & facilitating a complete transformation, with an evolution & effective transition to a unique niche meant for them, geared towards realizing their true potential in the process. Thus, transforming & turning ordinary stallions into truly game changers for the long-term.

CHAPTER X

LEADERSHIP PRESENCE AND THE POWER OF QUIET LEADERSHIP –OPERATING IN THE STEALTH MODE, INVISIBLE TO THE RADAR

The Discovery of Quiet Leaders

The concept of a low-key, quiet leader typically seems to be incongruous with the traditional concept of leadership figuratively. The quiet leader, working behind the scenes quietly & diligently, first got noticed at the turn of the century, almost two decades back by Jim Collins, while working on his book titled 'Good to Great' published in 2001, researching on what makes organizations great. This was also the theme of the HBR book, "Leading Quietly: An Unorthodox Guide to Doing the Right Thing", by Harvard professor Joseph L. Badaracco, published in 2002. However, it was the bestselling book, Quiet: The Power of Introverts in a World That Can't Stop Talking, by Susan Cain, which decrypted the code of the quiet, introverted leader, proved to be disruptive and brought the paradigm shift in 2012, while also bringing the much deserved & long overdue attention to the underrated introverts.

So, what is a typical quiet leader like? Professor Badaracco drew the silhouette of a quiet leader at work really well in one of his HBR interviews. He said, "They're not making high-stakes decisions. They're often not at the top of organizations. They don't have the spotlight and publicity on them. They think of themselves modestly; they often don't even think of themselves as leaders. But they are acting quietly, effectively, to basically make things somewhat better, sometimes much better than they would otherwise be. Sometimes a few people were aware of what they did; sometimes nobody is aware of what they did. There aren't medal ceremonies and often the people involved don't think they would deserve one if the medals were being given out. But often they're people, I found…in the cases I looked at carefully, who find that some situation or problem or difficulty affecting a person, affecting an organization, is really bothering them; it gets under their skin. While other people would say, "Hey, why are you getting carried away about this?", they care about it. They commit themselves and keep working tenaciously, so that over a period of time they find some ways to get stuff done."[75]

Susan Cain has opined that traditionally, mankind has typically been biased towards extroverted leaders, who tend to run the show while grabbing as much attention & limelight as they can, while eclipsing their introverted counterparts, in the process, who have been excellent leaders as well in their own quiet ways. Extroversion, thus, has almost been made synonymous with the very concept of leadership with the human brain & psyche conditioned effectively to believe so without looking at the fact that a number of great leaders have actually been introverted, who have, in turn, taken their organizations to the very top. The list of some of such great, quiet leaders includes, stalwarts, namely, Bill Gates, Warren Buffett, Abraham Lincoln, Albert Einstein, Larry Page, Steve Wozniak, Nelson Mandela and Steven Spielberg. The list also includes two more luminaries, the first man on moon, Neil Armstrong, and Phil Knight, founder & former chairman of Nike Inc., with both of them well known for their aversion to media attention.

Introverts vs. Extroverts – The Case for Introversion and Leadership

The barbed wire fencing and the iron curtain of sort, separating the introverts from the extroverts, was constructed originally by Carl Jung, over a century ago in 1910 with his type theory of personality. These two personality types exist & are positioned along the two opposite extremes of a typical bell curve depicting the personality continuum. Jung's personality types also form the basis of the Myers-Briggs Type Indicator (MBTI), the popular personality type inventory in psychology.

Introverts, with their typical strength of listening more than they talk, proves to be a great strength in the leadership role as they tend to listen more to the ideas generated by their team members, instead of being the big mouth in the room, always looking to make & prove his point. One of the best examples of its effectiveness comes from MSD himself. In the final of the 2011's ODI World Cup, the thought & idea of Dhoni batting up the order came from none other than the Little Master, Sachin Tendulkar, who revealed in a media interview[78] last year that it was him who had sent the message to Dhoni, via Sehwag, between the overs in that match, when India had been chasing. Dhoni listened, contemplated it and executed it perfectly to bring India home successfully with the cup.

Secondly, their ability to reflect upon the situations and get to insights & solutions; is another key weapon in their armoury. Apple's current leader,

Tim Cook, is a typical example of a quiet leader with his below the radar presence & unassuming leadership style which has been a major deviation from Steve Jobs' marked extraversion, flamboyance and charismatic leadership.

Key strengths of these quiet, introverted leaders, as captured superbly by an article[70, 71] published on Forbes, are as follows:

"They are better listeners

They embrace solitude, and what leader hasn't known loneliness?

They are wizards of preparation

They challenge themselves (and take that critical, extra second guess)

They dig deep into problems

They can be cool when others lose their cool" [70, 71].

The last point, regarding coolness under fire, has been the hallmark of the 'Captain Cool', MSD, which helps him not get distracted in the middle of the field, by the uproar, frenzy and cacophony of the spectators, and instead, stay focused on the game to come up with insights & ideas with his extraordinarily fast cricketing brain.

It also has helped him win multiple nail-biters and cliffhangers, through his cricketing years, which included 2 of his 3 ICC trophies, which were both won in the last over of the games, with the 2007's Twenty20 final and the 2013's Champions Trophy final, both decided, settled & won on the very last balls of these two high-stakes games. Further, their natural habit of thinking & reflecting, tends to make them improve their game incrementally almost autonomously, by generating insights & coming up with better ways of doing things, which then becomes a ripple effect, in turn, eventually becoming a team culture of seeking refinement & constant improvement based on the top-down approach.

Leadership is situational as well as contextual and there is no perfect leader or style for all types of organizations or for different stages of an organization along its evolutionary journey. An article published on Forbes captured it brilliantly, "When you've got a team of stars, they'll be best served by working under a quiet, introverted leader who respects their ideas and who is willing to let them shine. But if you have a team of passive people who prefer to be told what to do, they'll find such an introvert to be frustrating and uninspiring. And they'll often respond to a hotshot who talks a good game and who dominates the spotlight. They may even find themselves worshipping such a leader."[72]

MSD as the Quiet Leader

In the context of Indian Cricket, MSD emerged as that kind of quiet, introverted leader at the helm. Indian pace bowler, Ashish Nehra, provided a silhouette of the reticent Dhoni in one of his posts for media. He said about Dhoni, "Approachable but an introvert, who loved being in his own room, which was open to all. Probably the only cricketer who never went to anyone's room but would welcome juniors in. You could enter Mahi's room, pick up the phone, order room service, play video games, talk cricket, and if you had an issues with regards cricket, you could tell him. But yes, no outside gossip, no backbiting. He never let discussions drift that side. That's why he always wanted issues in the dressing room sorted there only. Nothing was meant for consumption of outside world."[82]

Team India, however, exactly needed that avatar of his, especially, during the 2011's World Cup campaign, which had a star-studded team, featuring stalwarts, some big egos and rising stars, all of whom had to be managed very skillfully & differentially, to get to the goal as well as the task at hand, without losing the way.

Prima donnas, as they are called, are team members who consider themselves as superior to others with their perceived special abilities & super powers and consider themselves to be indispensable for the team. They are good at their skill and that pumps their egos. A star-studded, self-directed team, usually is packed with domain specialist prima-donnas and managing it and guiding it adroitly to a directed goal can only be done successfully by a quiet leader at the top, who can do it seamlessly from behind by blending in perfectly, without ruffling feathers. This is what MSD did in 2011 and what Tim Cook has been doing inside Apple since taking over the reins from Steve Jobs. In the Indian context, the most appropriate analogy would be the stark contrast in leadership styles between the two former CEOs, Nanadan Nilekani and Vishal Sikka, of India's IT bellwether & giant, Infosys Technologies.

Evolution of MSD's Leadership Style – Radically Different Operating Contexts

MSD elaborated about leading a team of stalwarts and his leadership style in an interview given to bcci.tv in 2014. He had said, "The best thing about the senior players was that with their experience they had a lot of ideas and suggestions to give me. But more importantly, if I didn't agree with some things they said, I could tell them so. They were absolutely fine with it and after 10-15 minutes would again come up with a different idea or options and then leave it to me, give me a few deliveries to think about it and decide. That really gave me the comfort of knowing that I can be honest and straightforward with them without the fear of offending them.

Because of them I was able to be myself and develop my own style of captaincy."[84]

Additionally, what also needs to be seen is the sea change in his leadership style, way back in 2007's Twenty20 World Cup campaign, in which the team lacked its characteristic star power with the exclusion of some big names, and mostly had rookies charging in on most fronts. In that tournament, a flamboyant and firebrand MSD, led right from the front as a prancing mustang as the team needed it while effectively guiding his forces eventually to World Cup victory through some real tough battles.

This was much like how Steve Jobs had led Apple during the company's initial years. Susan Cain, too, in 'Quiet', mentions that, "With their natural ability to inspire, extroverted leaders are better at getting results from more passive workers."[73]

In essence, teams & organizations with passive members need extroversion based inspirational leadership, whereas, self-directed teams, comprising of domain specialists who are self-starters & go getters, simply need the nudge of a quiet leader & his quiet leadership.

Phil Knight has been a classic example of the same. He let his team be expressive, free & creative as he did not address their operational concerns by telling them. Rather he let them figure it out independently and get to the solutions on their own. In fact, the idea of naming the company as 'Nike', originated from his first employee who had seen it in his dream one night. The name was liked by the team but it didn't really click with Phil but he went with the team saying, "I guess it will grow on me."[79]

Seemingly, this major change in MSD's leadership style in 2011 was more of an evolution, as a person and as a leader, shaped by critical events on the personal front rather than being simply adaptation, as it has been duly sustained over the years since then. Another Indian captain, who has been the quiet leader on the cricket field in the 21st century, has been Rahul Dravid.

Personal & Psychological Aspect of Leadership – The 3P Model

The personal & psychological aspect of leadership has been covered excellently by the groundbreaking, "The Three Levels of Leadership" model or the 3P model, developed by James Scouller in 2011. The model has been classified as an integrated psychological theory of leadership. The theory states that the leaders, in addition, to bringing leadership to the organization; have to develop themselves as well, technically & psychologically, as leaders. Personal leadership forms the core of the three-tiered model represented by three concentric circles. Additionally, personal leadership forms the inner level of leadership while the private and public levels form the outer levels.

Scouller says regarding personal leadership, "At its heart is the leader's self-awareness, his progress toward self-mastery and technical competence, and his sense of connection with those around him. It's the inner core, the source, of a leader's outer leadership effectiveness."[69]

Scouller[69] states that the personal leadership level has the following three aspects to it:-

1. Technical Knowhow and Skill

2. Attitude towards Other People

3. Psychological Self-Mastery

Technical knowhow comes under domain leadership while attitude towards other people broadly comes under humble leadership with core focus on developing an attitude of service towards the followers and the creation of a meaningful, collective & mutually shared vision.

Regarding psychological self-mastery, Scouller has argued that "self-mastery is the key to growing one's leadership presence, building trusting relationships with followers and enabling behavioral flexibility as circumstances change, while staying connected to one's core values (that is, while remaining authentic)."[69]

Leadership Presence & the 3P Model

Presence, as per the 3P model, is developed by practicing personal leadership with Scouller having outlined seven qualities[69] of presence as follows:-

1. Personal power – Command over one's thoughts, feelings & actions
2. High, real self-esteem
3. The drive to learn, grow & be more
4. Balance between an energetic sense of purpose with a concern for the service of others and respect for their free will
5. Intuition
6. Being in the now
7. Inner peace of mind and a sense of fulfillment

Even a cursory look at the qualities of presence, as mentioned by Scouller, makes it self-evident that it quintessentially is a terrain typically favouring & skewed towards introverts, as most of the qualities, especially, intuition, the drive to learn, balance and inner peace of mind & fulfillment etc. are almost like second nature to them.

All of these are very naturally done by introverts & are almost cakewalk for them while for extreme extroverts, being able to look inwards, itself is like descending down the rabbit hole and has to be a learned ability.

The natural ability for extroverts in fact is to exude confidence & charisma, with or sometimes even without substance, or the foundation of presence. The pathway for leading others, thus, starts with an inward journey. The key, thus, is to get to the zone right in the middle of these two extremes, described as ambiverts, to get the best of both worlds by cultivating balance; a view which Carl Jung also believed was essential to reach the goal of self-realization.

MSD & Presence

Presence, thus, is a way deeper construct than it seems on the surface and creates a much broader ripple effect on the very same surface than ever realized...as demonstrated effectively by MSD on the cricket field.

A recent comment from KL Rahul, given to Forbes India in an interview, perfectly captures MSD's quintessential leadership and what it meant for his teammates. Rahul said, "The minute anybody says captain, the first name which comes into anybody's mind from our generation is MS Dhoni. We have all played under him. Yes, he has won a lot of tournaments, done amazing things for the country but I think the biggest achievement that as a captain you can have is respect of your teammates."[101]

He further added with a mighty statement in itself, "You know, any of us would take a bullet for him without a second thought..."[101]

The ex-coach wants to 'go to war' with him and the former teammates, more than eager to even 'take a bullet for him', just goes to show his presence, leadership and the magic. This why MSD has been synonymous with captaincy & leadership and will always remain special & a legend of the game for time immemorial…

The Power of Quiet Leadership

The advent of the quiet leader to the fore paved the way for the formal emergence of Quiet Leadership, as a leadership philosophy and model, developed by Dr. David Rock, a neuroscience researcher, who coined the term NeuroLeadership, back in 2007. The same has also been outlined as a six-step process in his book, Quiet Leadership, published in 2007.

Quiet Leadership is based on neuroscience principles and, essentially, is about 'asking' instead of 'telling', a key departure from the traditional way, to bring about a transformational change. This is based on the principle outlined by Sir John Whitmore, former British racing driver and a pre-eminent thinker in the domain of leadership development & organizational change and the creator of GROW model. He had outlined the secret to the 'Asking' philosophy in his bestselling book, Coaching for Performance, as, "To tell denies or negates another's intelligence. To ask honours it."[74]

It is about making them get to learn fishing for themselves by asking, 'how to', rather than telling them 'This is how to fish' or 'fishing for' them. The emphasis on 'Asking' is based on the premise that every individual in his role is a domain specialist, who knows his role best and knows, either consciously or sub-consciously, how to improve his game further and needs just a nudge or structured facilitated thinking rather than being told outright. It is about making the team members or employees think in a solution-focused, structured manner to get to insights & actionable alternatives with the process facilitated by the leader based on asking and listening.

This also has to do with research into the concept of excellence & perfection-seeking, as mentioned earlier as well, which prescribes, that the pursuit of improvement, excellence & perfection-seeking; has to done by the individual with intrinsic motivation for motivation & outcomes. If it is done, based on social prescription or is other-oriented with extrinsic motivation, it only leads to development of anxiety and confidence issues. For instance, media's constant pestering of a player over his technique or style of play would only cause insecurity, shake his confidence and in turn would reflect in his on-field performances.

Quiet leadership, thus, has been a coaching model and a toolkit for being the quiet leader in any given scenario with relevance & application across all three levels of leadership in an organization.

Learning Principle:

Leadership is situational as well as contextual and there is no perfect leader or style for all types of organizations or for different stages of an organization along its evolutionary journey. Teams & organizations with passive members need extroversion based inspirational leadership, whereas, self-directed teams, comprising of domain specialists, who are self-starters & go getters, simply need the nudge of a quiet leader & the subtle power of his quiet leadership.

That's it folks…

On a concluding note, leadership, as any other domain, is a constant work in progress with its conception as a state of static perfection merely being a conceptual fallacy. Leaders, like everyone, have to be on their toes on the same evolutionary learning path to become an even better version of themselves every today than yesterday ad infinitum with discipline & commitment to the very end to be truly victorious meaningfully in career as well as life.

Let's stay mobile and keep walking nimbly…

We all have got to remember that greatness can never be chased…Those who have attempted, with their perceived super powers, have crashed mid-air, extinguished and simply disappeared without a trace… It is all about becoming truly worthy & deserving and is an inward journey rather than outward…

Wherever and whichever stage of the journey you may be on…

Wish you the very best…Hang on and remember that nobody is perfect, it's OK to make mistakes and it's mostly about the journey…

So, Let's Keep Walking and Keep Evolving…

Here's to MSD as there has never been anyone like him and will never be…

Also, to the true Leader in all of us whether Latent or already Discovered…

Over & Out!

Bibliography

1. 'I knew that even 350 might not be enough' – Dhoni, ESPN cricinfo News, April 05, 2005, Chandrahas Choudhary, Wisden Asia Cricket Magazine
https://www.espncricinfo.com/story/a-man-possessed-143844

2. 'A man possessed', ESPN cricinfo News, April 05, 2005, Chandrahas Choudhary, Wisden Asia Cricket Magazine
https://www.espncricinfo.com/story/a-man-possessed-143844

3. ESPN Cricinfo, Statistics,
https://stats.espncricinfo.com/ci/engine/records/index.html

4. Bagehot (15 June 2017). "Jeremy Corbyn, Entrepreneur". *The Economist*. p. 53. Retrieved 23 June 2017. The most influential business idea of recent years is Clayton Christensen's theory of disruptive innovation."

5. "When Greatbatch went gonzo", The Cricket Monthly, ESPN Cricinfo, February 2015, By Dylan Cleaver
https://www.thecricketmonthly.com/story/825039/dylan-cleaver--when-greatbatch-went-gonzo

6. "2003 World Cup final: If only India had chosen to bat first...", Mint, May 05, 2017 By
https://www.livemint.com/Sundayapp/4V5GYZgqJJioqFKXSfYFJI/2003-World-Cup-final-If-only-India-had-chosen-to-bat-first.html

7. "The Indians in New Zealand, 2002-03", Wisden, ESPN Cricinfo, Lawrence Booth
https://www.espncricinfo.com/wisdenalmanack/content/story/156038.html

8. "The bowlers have responded well – Dhoni", ESPN Cricinfo, September 23, 2007, By S. Rajesh in Durban,
https://www.espncricinfo.com/story/the-bowlers-have-responded-well-dhoni-312148

9. "Extreme Ownership", by Jocko Willink and Leif Babin, 2015, St. Martin's Press,
ISBN 13: 978-1250067050
https://www.amazon.com/Extreme-Ownership-U-S-Navy-SEALs/dp/1250067057

10. "Love the shot of MS Dhoni's 2011 World Cup-winning six: Jos Buttler", The Times of India, IANS, May 18, 2021
https://timesofindia.indiatimes.com/sports/cricket/news/love-the-shot-of-ms-dhonis-2011-world-cup-winning-six-jos-buttler/articleshow/82733752.cms

11. "MS Dhoni delays return to Ranchi till all his CSK teammates depart", Indian Express, Devendra Pandey, May 08, 2021
https://indianexpress.com/article/sports/ipl/ms-dhoni-delays-return-to-ranchi-till-all-his-csk-teammates-depart-7303778/

12. "IPL 2020: MS Dhoni Admits He Was Not Able To Middle Lot Of Deliveries As CSK Suffer Third Straight Defeat", PTI, October 03, 2020

https://www.outlookindia.com/website/story/sports-news-ipl-2020-ms-dhoni-admits-he-was-not-able-to-middle-lot-of-deliveries-as-csk-suffer-third-straight-defeat/361396

13. "Skunk Works: A Personal Memoir of my Years at Lockheed", By Ben R. Rich & Leo Janos, Back Bay Books, pp. 128-129, ISBN 978-0-316-74300-6

14. Weber, Maximillan. *Theory of Social and Economic Organization.* Chapter: "The Nature of Charismatic Authority and its Routinization" translated by A. R. Anderson and Talcott Parsons, 1947. Originally published in 1922 in German under the title *Wirtschaft und Gesellschaft chapter III, § 10*

15. "Why the Military Produces Great Leaders", Tom Kolditz, Harvard Business Review, February 06, 2009

https://hbr.org/2009/02/why-the-military-produces-grea

16. "India beat Sri-Lanka: India wins by 7 wickets", ESPN Cricinfo, Match Summary, Report

https://www.espncricinfo.com/series/commonwealth-bank-series-2011-12-518940/india-vs-sri-lanka-11th-match-518966/live-cricket-score

17. Burns, J.M, (1978), Leadership, N.Y, Harper and Row

18. Bass, B. M,(1985), Leadership and Performance, N.Y. Free Press

19. Shoe Dog: A Memoir by the Creator of Nike – By Phil Knight, Published by Scribner,

https://www.amazon.com/Shoe-Dog-Memoir-Creator-Nike-ebook/dp/B0176M1A44/ref=tmm_kin_swatch_0?_encoding=UTF8&qid=&sr=#detailBullets_feature_div

20. "The Starfish and the Spider: the unstoppable power of leaderless organizations". By Ori Brafman, Rod. A. Beckstrom. 2006.. New York: Penguin Group. https://www.amazon.com/Starfish-Spider-Unstoppable-Leaderless-Organizations/dp/B015QKUC6K

21. "Johnson, Clarence L. 'Kelly' & Smith, Maggie (1985). "Kelly: More Than My Share of It All". Foreword by Leo P. Geary. Washington, D.C.: Smithsonian Institution. ISBN 978-0874745641. https://www.amazon.com/Kelly-Johnson-Clarence-Maggie-Hardcover/dp/B011MFAYWU

22. The Skunk Works Legacy, Lockheed Martin Corporation, https://www.lockheedmartin.com/en-us/who-we-are/business-areas/aeronautics/skunkworks/skunk-works-origin-story.html

23. "Johnson's hunch becomes a Lockheed Signature", Lockheed Martin Corporation, https://www.lockheedmartin.com/en-us/news/features/history/electra.html

24. "Clarence "Kelly" Johnson: Architect of the Air", Lockheed Martin Corporation, https://www.lockheedmartin.com/en-us/news/features/history/johnson.html

25. "Grit: The Power of Passion & Perseverance", By Angela Duckworth, Scribner Book Company, ISBN 978-1501111105 https://www.amazon.com/Grit-Passion-Perseverance-Angela-Duckworth/dp/1501111108/ref=sr_1_1?ie=UTF8&qid=1447597032&sr=8-1&keywords=Grit+Angela+Duckworth

26. "The resident of MS Dhoni's original Ranchi house gives out interesting details". CricTracker, Umaima, March 16, 2017 https://www.crictracker.com/the-resident-of-ms-dhonis-original-ranchi-house-gives-out-interesting-details/

27. "How MS Dhoni helped cricketer Indrani Roy Grow as a Wicketkeeper", Sportstar, By Shayan Acharya, May 15, 2021 https://sportstar.thehindu.com/cricket/indrani-roy-interview-ms-dhoni-suggestions-wicketkeeping-liluah-taniya-bhatia/article34564792.ece

28. "Sometimes I miss MS Dhoni's guidance, says Kuldeep Yadav", The Times of India, IANS, May 12, 2021 https://timesofindia.indiatimes.com/sports/cricket/sometimes-i-miss-ms-dhonis-guidance-says-kuldeep-yadav/articleshow/82568907.cms

29. "MS Dhoni Made me Powerplay Bowler: Deepak Chahar Credits CSK Captain for his Impressive IPL Returns", India.com Sports Desk, May 22, 2021 https://www.india.com/sports/cricket-ms-dhoni-made-me-powerplay-bowler-deepak-chahar-credits-csk-captain-for-his-impressive-ipl-returns-4683153/

30. Koepp, M., Gunn, R., Lawrence, A. *et al.* Evidence for striatal dopamine release during a video game. *Nature* **393,** 266–268 (1998). https://doi.org/10.1038/30498 https://www.nature.com/articles/30498

31. "My last WhatsApp with Jagdish Khattar and how it defined 'Mr. Maruti'", The Times of India, Malini Goyal, April 28, 2021.

https://timesofindia.indiatimes.com/blogs/therovingeye/my-last-whatsapp-with-jagdish-khattar-how-it-defined-mr-maruti/

32. "If there's commitment, that's victory for me", ESPN Cricinfo, March 24, 2008, By Siddhartha Vaidyanathan and Nagraj Gollapudi https://www.espncricinfo.com/story/if-there-s-commitment-that-s-victory-for-me-343750

33. "The 21 Irrefutable Laws of Leadership", John C. Maxwell, Harper Collins, ISBN-10 : 0785288376, https://www.amazon.in/21-Irrefutable-Laws-Leadership-Follow/dp/0785288376

34. Ethical Challenges in Contemporary Conflict: The Afghanistan and Iraq Cases, Centre for the Study of Professional Military Ethics, U.S. Naval Academy https://www.usna.edu/Ethics/_files/documents/MattisPg1-28_Final.pdf

35. "15 Things Mattis Taught Me About Real Leadership", Task & Purpose, By Joe Plenzler, December 20, 2016 https://taskandpurpose.com/leadership/gen-mattis-no-mad-dog-told-1st-marine-division-proves/

36. "One Bullet Away: The Making of a US Marine Officer", By Nathaniel Fick, W&N, Published March 2007, ISBN 978-0753821879 https://www.amazon.in/One-Bullet-Away-making-Officer/dp/0753821877

37. Brain Reward Pathways, Neuroscience Department Laboratories, Icahn School of Medicine at Mount Sinai. http://neuroscience.mssm.edu/nestler/brainRewardpathways.html

38. "Dopamine impacts your willingness to work", Research News @Vanderbilt, By David Salisbury, May 01, 2012 https://news.vanderbilt.edu/2012/05/01/dopamine-impacts-your-willingness-to-work/

39. Dopamine and Addiction: Separating Myths & Facts, Healthline, By Crystal Raypole, April 30, 2019 https://www.healthline.com/health/dopamine-addiction

40. "Michael Clarke confirms black armband was in memory of Phil Hughes after ICC Cricket World Cup Final", Cricket Country, By Agence France-Presse, March 29, 2015. https://www.cricketcountry.com/news/michael-clarke-confirms-black-armband-was-in-memory-of-phil-hughes-after-icc-cricket-world-cup-2015-final-270387

41. How the West Indies Cricket team overcame administrative problems to become World Champions, Sportskeeda, April 04, 2016, By Unaima Saeed https://www.sportskeeda.com/cricket/west-indies-cricket-team-overcame-administrative-problems-world-champions

42. "We versus them" – Andre Fletcher reveals West Indies team was motivated to win T20 WC 2016 because of dispute with the board. Sportskeeda, Vinay Chhabaria, May 20, 2021 https://www.sportskeeda.com/cricket/news-we-versus-them-andre-fletcher-reveals-west-indies-team-motivated-win-t20-wc-2016-dispute-board

43. Caribbean Cricket Podcast, Episode 41, Preview #2, https://youtu.be/9ligd1CpsvU

44. "10 Years of 2011 World Cup Win: We wanted to win for Sachin Tendulkar, says Yuvraj Singh", Zee Media Bureau,

Devadyuti Das, April 02, 2021

https://zeenews.india.com/cricket/10-years-of-2011-world-cup-win-we-wanted-to-win-for-sachin-tendulkar-says-yuvraj-singh-2352228.html

45. "Are Dolphins Reciprocal Altruists?", Richard C. Connor & Kenneth S. Norris, The University of Chicago Press Journals, The American Naturalist, Volume 119, Number 3 https://www.journals.uchicago.edu/doi/pdf/10.1086/283915

46. Altruistic Behavior: mapping responses in the brain, Megan M Filkowski, R Nick Cochran, Brian W Haas, NCBI, PMC, U.S. National Library of Medicine, National Institutes of Health
https://www.ncbi.nlm.nih.gov/pmc/articles/PMC5456281/#R6

47. The Phrase Finder,
https://www.phrases.org.uk/meanings/different-strokes-for-different-folks.html

48. Jhoon Rhee, Father of American Taekwondo, Biography
http://www.jhoonrhee.com/bio7.html

49. "#2 Be water, my friend", Bruce Lee, Podcast-Blog
https://brucelee.com/podcast-blog/2016/7/20/2-be-water-my-friend

50. Bruce Lee, The 'Lost' Interview, The Pierre Berton Show, 1971 https://www.youtube.com/watch?v=eVX2JXX4sF8

51. "Once Rejected by Railways, Dhoni wins maiden match against them", Hindustan Times, By Prabhash C. Jha, December 17, 2015
https://www.hindustantimes.com/cricket/once-rejected-by-

railways-dhoni-wins-maiden-match-against-them/story-Ynb6cMCFGVmOv4Lz2p8tSM.html

52. "MS Dhoni's Wicket-Keeping Style Should Not be Aped by Youngsters: Syed Kirmani", Outlook Magazine, Outlook Web Bureau, October 09, 2018 https://www.outlookindia.com/website/story/ms-dhonis-wicket-keeping-style-should-not-be-aped-by-youngsters-syed-kirmani/318018

53. 'MSD, the inspiration behind keeper-captains', The Hindu, PTI, April 11, 2021 https://www.thehindu.com/sport/cricket/msd-the-inspiration-behind-keeper-captains/article34297121.ece

54. 'You almost ended my son's career', Yuvraj reveals what Stuart Broad's father told him after hitting six sixes. myKhel, By Chitrangada Dc, April 27, 2020 https://www.mykhel.com/cricket/you-almost-ended-my-son-s-career-yuvraj-reveals-what-stuart-broad-s-father-told-him-hitting-sixes-142430.html?story=2

55. "Rohit Sharma reveals how MS Dhoni helped transform his career", NDTV Sports Eng, January 11, 2017, Edited by Dattaraj Thaly https://sports.ndtv.com/cricket/rohit-sharma-reveals-how-ms-dhoni-helped-transform-his-career-1647710

56. "Yuvraj Singh pays tribute to MS Dhoni as Captain, Shares Video Highlighting Friendship", NDTV Sports Eng, January 11, 2017, Abhishek Mahajan https://sports.ndtv.com/cricket/yuvraj-singh-pays-tribute-to-

ms-dhoni-as-captain-shares-video-highlighting-friendship-1647499

57. "Had to beg & plead for opening slot" – Sachin Tendulkar recounts his baptism with fire as ODI opener in 1994, CricTracker, September 26, 2019
https://www.crictracker.com/had-to-beg-and-plead-for-opening-slot-sachin-tendulkar-recounts-his-baptism-with-fire-as-odi-opener-in-1994/

58. "Jadeja Names Dhoni as the Key Person for his Transformation", Times of Sports, June 01, 2021
https://www.timesofsports.com/cricket/news/jadeja-praises-dhoni/

59. "How Ravindra Jadeja made the leap", HT Mint, By Chetan Narula, Feb 05, 2014
https://www.livemint.com/Leisure/BrUjVnQm8pZNw3HSsu6UEO/How-Ravindra-Jadeja-made-the-leap.html

60. "Sachin volunteered to bat at No. 4 so that Sehwag can open in ODIs: Former India keeper Ajay Ratra", Hindustan Times, July 16, 2020, By Aritra Mukherjee,
https://www.hindustantimes.com/cricket/exclusive-sachin-volunteered-to-bat-at-no-4-so-that-sehwag-can-open-in-odis-former-india-keeper-ajay-ratra/story-TelO8nkJT08eSN9HQD4bfK.html

61. "What is the importance of the Nürburgring for car testing?", Lamborghini Palm Beach
https://www.lamborghinipalmbeach.com/blog/what-is-the-nurburgring/

62. "Understanding Michael Porter: The Essential Guide to Competition and Strategy", Joan Magretta, Harvard Business Review Press, 2011, ISBN13 978-1422160596 https://www.amazon.in/Understanding-Michael-Porter-Margretta/dp/1422160599

63. "Innovation Lessons from Pixar: An interview with Oscar-Winning director Brad Bird", McKinsey Quarterly, By Hayagreeva Rao, Robert Sutton, and Allen P. Webb, April 01, 2008, https://www.mckinsey.com/business-functions/strategy-and-corporate-finance/our-insights/innovation-lessons-from-pixar-an-interview-with-oscar-winning-director-brad-bird#

64. "Grace under fire", ESPN CricInfo, By Dileep Premachandran, Sep 26, 2007 https://www.espncricinfo.com/story/top-performer-mahendra-singh-dhoni-312575

65. "I would go to war with Dhoni by my side: Gary Kirsten", DNA India, By Vijay Tagore, June 18, 2011, https://www.dnaindia.com/sports/report-i-would-go-to-war-with-dhoni-by-my-side-gary-kirsten-1556275

66. Wasielewski, P. (1985). The Emotional Basis of Charisma. *Symbolic Interaction, 8*(2), 207-222. doi:10.1525/si.1985.8.2.207 https://www.jstor.org/stable/10.1525/si.1985.8.2.207

67. "What is charisma? Body Language Quick Takes #9", Forbes, By Nick Morgan, Oct 06, 2011 https://www.forbes.com/sites/nickmorgan/2011/10/06/what-is-charisma-body-language-quick-takes-9/?sh=3380ab4e130f

68. "The Most Charismatic General Ever?" Forbes, By Nick Morgan, June 20, 2013 https://www.forbes.com/sites/nickmorgan/2013/06/20/the-most-charismatic-general-ever/?sh=64dc4c7e4389

69. Scouller, J. (2011). The Three Levels of Leadership: How to Develop Your Leadership Presence, Knowhow and Skill. Cirencester: Management Books 2000., ISBN 9781852526818

70. "The real reason Apple's Tim Cook has been underestimated", The Mac Observer, By John Martellaro, September 11, 2014 https://www.macobserver.com/tmo/article/the-real-reason-apples-tim-cook-has-been-underestimated

71. "Why introverts can be great leaders?", By Rahul Sinha, Linked In, September 1, 2014 https://www.linkedin.com/pulse/20140901044830-169955770-why-introverts-are-better-leaders

72. "That moment when a quiet leader outshines the loud ones", Forbes, By Rob Asghar, August 11, 2015 https://www.forbes.com/sites/robasghar/2015/08/11/that-moment-when-a-quiet-leader-outshines-the-loud-ones/?sh=22b545bf1a7b

73. "Quiet: The power of introverts in a world that can't stop talking", By Susan Cain, Published by Penguin UK, 2013, ISBN 978-0141029191 https://www.amazon.in/Quiet-power-introverts-world-talking/dp/0141029196

74. Coaching for Performance: The Principles and Practice of Coaching and Leadership, By Sir John Whitmore, Nicholas Brealey Publishing, 2010, https://www.amazon.in/Coaching-Performance-Principles-Leadership-Professionals-ebook/dp/B01HPVHM0C#detailBullets_feature_div

75. "The Quiet Leader – and How to be One", Harvard Business School, Working Knowledge – Business Research for Business Leaders – Research and Ideas, By Martha Lagace, February 11, 2002 https://hbswk.hbs.edu/item/the-quiet-leaderand-how-to-be-one

76. "Dhoni never insulted us, he told media we are slow fielders: Virender Sehwag", Hindustan Times, September 06, 2020 https://www.hindustantimes.com/cricket/dhoni-

never-consulted-us-he-told-media-we-are-slow-fielders-virender-sehwag/story-1Q8ynjX3OaPHpV7zlOnH2J.html

77. "Jim Mattis once pulled Christmas duty for a young Marine – and it's the perfect holiday story", CNBC make it, By Vanna Le, https://www.cnbc.com/2018/12/21/why-jim-mattis-once-pulled-christmas-duty-for-a-young-marine.html

78. "It was Sachin! Tendulkar reveals it was he who prompted MS Dhoni's WC2011 Batting Switch", RepublicWorld.com, By Prachi Mankani, April 05, 2020 https://www.republicworld.com/sports-news/cricket-news/sachin-tendulkars-revelation-about-dhonis-position-in-2011-world-cup.html

79. "5 Leadership Lessons from the Man that Created Nike", Coach Ayers Performance Blog, https://www.coachayers.com/blog/5-leadership-lessons-from-the-man-that-created-nike#

80. Portrait of an icon: Tony Adams, Football 365, By Daniel Storey, July 20, 2016. https://www.football365.com/news/portrait-of-an-icon-tony-adams

81. "When MS Dhoni Drove Team Bus in Nagpur During 2008 Test Series Against Australia", News 18, Last Updated: August 18, 2020, CricketNEXT Staff https://www.news18.com/cricketnext/news/ms-dhoni-retires-when-ms-dhoni-drove-team-bus-in-nagpur-during-2008-test-series-against-australia-2796803.html

82. "MS Dhoni's Doors were always open , but never for gossip or backbiting" – Ashish Nehra", News18, August 17, 2020, PTI. https://www.news18.com/cricketnext/news/ms-dhonis-doors-were-always-open-but-never-for-gossip-or-backbiting-ashish-nehra-2795633.html

83. 'On the offside, first there is God, then Dada': 20 quotes that prove the cricketing world is overawed by Sourav Ganguly, News 18, July 08, 2014 https://www.news18.com/news/buzz/on-the-offside-first-there-is-god-then-dada-20-quotes-that-prove-the-

cricketing-world-is-overawed-by-sourav-ganguly-700317.html

84. MS Dhoni Talks about Art of Leadership, India Times, July 08, 2014, https://www.indiatimes.com/sports/cricket/ms-dhoni-my-gut-feeling-is-driven-by-experience-logic-159979.html

85. MS Dhoni's captaincy changed perception of leadership among captains: Lakshmipathy Balaji. The Times of India, By IANS. August 20, 2020 https://timesofindia.indiatimes.com/sports/cricket/ipl/top-stories/ms-dhonis-captaincy-changed-perception-of-leadership-among-captains-lakshmipathy-balaji/articleshow/77692287.cms

86. "TOI Exclusive: Virat Kohli and Ravi Shastri on World Cup, MS Dhoni, Bumrah and More", The Times of India, May 15, 2019, By K Shriniwas Rao, https://timesofindia.indiatimes.com/sports/cricket/icc-world-cup/icc-world-cup-2019-god-filters-everyone-says-virat-kohli/articleshow/69334767.cms

87. "From Virat Kohli to Steve Waugh: A look at 5 most successful captains in history of Test cricket" Timesnownews.com, By Siddharth Thakur, June 02, 2021 https://www.timesnownews.com/sports/cricket/article/virat-kohli-steve-waugh-kane-williamson-ricky-ponting-5-most-successful-captains-in-history-of-test-cricket-icc-world-test-championship-final/764935

88. "MS Dhoni Speech: Be Honest & Take Risks", https://www.englishspeecheschannel.com/english-speeches/ms-dhoni-speech/

89. "One has a lot of trophies, other built the team': India keeper on difference between MS Dhoni and Sourav Ganguly". Hindustan Times, July 19, 2020 https://www.hindustantimes.com/cricket/one-has-lot-of-trophies-other-built-the-team-india-keeper-on-difference-between-ms-dhoni-and-sourav-ganguly-as-captain/story-eRu0WrSBGMALR9hvYoRmuJ.html

90. "My Biggest Legacy: Sourav Ganguly identifies six match-winners", Hindustan Times, June 17, 2020 https://www.hindustantimes.com/cricket/that-was-my-biggest-legacy-sourav-ganguly-identifies-players-who-helped-india-win-2011-world-cup/story-5P9aKLiYLe0ES3k0N7LRqL.html

91. "Sourav Ganguly: Indian Cricket is like football in Brazil", Sportstar, June 13, 2020 https://sportstar.thehindu.com/cricket/sourav-ganguly-virat-kohli-rahul-dravid-indian-cricket-kumble-football-brazil/article31821839.ece

92. "Here's what Rahul Dravid told Irfan Pathan and MS Dhoni after the 2007 World Cup Exit", Cricket Addictor, By Asyushman Vishwanathan, May 31, 2020 https://cricketaddictor.com/cricket/rahul-dravid-irfan-pathan-ms-dhoni/

93. "Success breeds success, study confirms", April 28, 2014, Stony Brook University https://www.sciencedaily.com/releases/2014/04/140428154838.htm

94. "Why Humble Leaders Make the Best Leaders", Forbes.com, By Jeff Hyman, October 31, 2018 https://www.forbes.com/sites/jeffhyman/2018/10/31/humility/?sh=5dcca461c800

95. "IPL 2021: Dhoni praises his players who are yet to get chance", Xtra Time, By Subhabrata Mukherjee, April 29, 2021 https://xtratime.in/ipl-2021-dhoni-praises-his-players-from-reserve-bench/

96. "The night Oscar Valdez shocked the experts", maxBoxing.com, March 05, 2021, By John J. Raspanti https://www.maxboxing.com/news/news/the-night-oscar-valdez-shocked-the-experts

97. Lee, Bruce (September 1971), "Liberate Yourself From Classical Karate", Black Belt Magazine, Rainbow Publications, Inc., vol. 9 no. 9, p. 24.

98. "MS Dhoni's 7 rules of success", January 05, 2017, By Abhishek Mahalpure,

https://abhishekmahalpure.wordpress.com/2017/01/05/m-s-dhonis-7-rules-of-success/

99. "Why You Should Take the Blame", Harvard Business Review, By Peter Bregman, April 08, 2013, https://hbr.org/2013/04/why-you-should-take-the-blame.html

100. "Seabiscuit vs. War Admiral: the horse race that stopped the nation" By Thom Loverro, The Guardian, November 01, 2013 https://www.theguardian.com/sport/2013/nov/01/seabiscuit-war-admiral-horse-race-1938-pimlico

101. 'We will take a bullet for him': KL Rahul's big statement on MS Dhoni, DNA India, DNA Web Team, Editor: Anshul Gupta, DNA Webdesk, July 03, 2021 https://www.dnaindia.com/cricket/report-we-will-take-a-bullet-for-him-without-a-second-thought-kl-rahul-s-big-statement-on-mahendra-singh-ms-dhoni-2898692

102. "People didn't understand MS Dhoni's gut feel…': KL Rahul on reasons behind CSK captain's success. By HT Sports Desk, Hindustan Times, May 18, 2023 https://www.hindustantimes.com/cricket/people-didn-t-understand-ms-dhonis-gut-feel-kl-rahul-on-reasons-behind-csk-captains-success-101684348444683.html

ABOUT THE AUTHORS

RAJAT NARANG

Rajat Narang is the Co-Founder and Partner of a niche Research Firm pivoted on the Global Aerospace & Defense Industry since 2009 apart from being a serial Author, active Podcaster and a Global E-Commerce Entrepreneur.

He has authored over 2000+ syndicated research reports and has authored multiple books on Commercial & Military Aviation & Leadership with the end users of his reports have been senior executives of leading A&D Industry OEMs, led by Airbus, Boeing, Bombardier, Embraer, Gulfstream, Dassault, Textron Aviation and their supplier base, including, engine OEMs and T1 suppliers such as GE Aviation, Rolls Royce, Pratt & Whitney, Safran & Spirit Aerosystems. His reports have also been leveraged by the U.S. Air Force, U S Navy & top global defense primes, including, Lockheed Martin Corporation, BAE Systems, General Dynamics Land Systems, Raytheon Technologies and Korean Aerospace Industries (KAI).

His educational background includes a Masters in Business Administration (MBA) in International Business with Business Strategy as the core pivot followed by a Masters in Political Science with specialization in International Relations. Being truly passionate about Naval Aviation and having almost made the cut to be a Naval Aviator following a selection by the Naval Academy in the late 1990s, A&D continues to be the core pivot of his professional pursuits even to this day.

His podcasts "Birds of Fray: Top Gun Maverick" and "M.S. Dhoni: Leadership Masterclass from the Master of the Craft" are available on most leading global platforms, including, Amazon Music, Spotify, Apple Podcasts & Google Podcasts and have a substantial following.

Bitten early by the A&D & Strategy bugs while growing up, he has been avidly & actively following, tracking & pursuing them for over 2+ decades now.

BHUMIKA CHANDRA

Bhumika Chandra has been a **Motivational Speaker** and **Learning & Development (L&D) professional**. She has been an **Independent Soft Skills Trainer**; Neuroscience based Life, Management & Leadership **Coach** and a **Workplace Psychologist**, in addition, to being a **Retail and e-Retail Service Quality Auditor/Evaluator in a career spanning almost 2 decades**. She is the Co-Founder & Partner of a niche, Research Firm pivoted on A&D. She is also the life member of Indian Society for Training & Development (ISTD).

Her educational background includes a Bachelor of **Computer Applications**, Master's education in **Business Management**, An advanced diploma in **Training & Development**; Masters in **Psychology** with specialization in **Workplace, Industrial & Organizational Psychology** followed by a certification in Neuroscience based **Coaching**.

She has also written a poetry book, titled "Phoenix Junction – The Cauldron of Inner Alchemy" themed   on resilience.

She almost made the cut to be an Aviator with the Indian Air Force (IAF) having cleared the Pilot Aptitude Battery Test (PABT) and a selection for the Air Force Academy in the early 2000s.

Other Titles from the Authors

Rajat Narang

1. Airbus vs. Boeing: Aviation's Dramatic Narrow-Body Cliffhanger Spanning 3+ Decades! - Strategy Perspective - I (Airbus vs. Boeing: Strategy Perspective - Book 1)

   https://www.amazon.in/Airbus-vs-Boeing-Narrow-Body-Cliffhanger-ebook/dp/B08HKJ7TF3

2. Airbus vs. Boeing: Aviation's Dramatic Narrow-Body Cliffhanger Spanning 3+ Decades! - Strategy Perspective - II (Airbus vs. Boeing: Strategy Perspective - Book 2)

   https://www.amazon.in/Airbus-vs-Boeing-Narrow-Body-Cliffhanger-ebook/dp/B08KQGSLC9

AVIATION'S DRAMATIC NARROW-
BODY CLIFFHANGER SPANNING 3+
DECADES...

Strategy Perspective - II

RAJAT NARANG

Bhumika Chandra

Phoenix Junction – The Cauldron of Inner Alchemy

https://www.amazon.in/Phoenix-Junction-Cauldron-Alchemy-Resilience-ebook/dp/B08Y757Y5P

www.ingramcontent.com/pod-product-compliance
Lightning Source LLC
Chambersburg PA
CBHW070641220526
45466CB00001B/246